BEYOND THE TITLE

Be Strong,

"WHISKY IS GOOD PROOFING WATER. TELLS YOU WHO'S REAL AND WHO ISN'T."
T. SHELBY

Storms!

Winter is good
without water.
Tell me who
head and who
sent?
1. Shelby

BEYOND THE TITLE

WOMEN IN JOURNALISM & MEDIA

LAUREN BANNISTER

NEW DEGREE PRESS

COPYRIGHT © 2020 LAUREN BANNISTER

All rights reserved.

BEYOND THE TITLE
WOMEN IN JOURNALISM & MEDIA

ISBN   978-1-63676-598-3   *Paperback*
        978-1-63676-247-0   *Kindle Ebook*
        978-1-63676-248-7   *Ebook*

> "Words have power.
> TV has power.
> My pen has power."
>
> —SHONDA RHIMES

CONTENTS

INTRODUCTION		1
PART 1.	**THE INDUSTRY**	**9**
CHAPTER 1.	WHAT IS JOURNALISM?	11
CHAPTER 2.	MULTI-MEDIA JOURNALISM	17
CHAPTER 3.	FINDING A FIELD OF VISION	27
PART 2.	**THE FOUNDATIONS**	**35**
CHAPTER 4.	YOU HAVE TO START SOMEWHERE	37
CHAPTER 5.	EXPAND YOUR VISION	51
CHAPTER 6.	VALUES BUILD A BRAND	61
CHAPTER 7.	BET ON YOURSELF	73
PART 3.	**THE ADVICE**	**83**
CHAPTER 8.	BE COURAGEOUS	85
CHAPTER 9.	BE CURIOUS	97
CHAPTER 10.	BE CONFIDENT	109
CHAPTER 11.	BE VALUABLE	121

| PART 4. | WHAT TO DO NOW | **131** |

CHAPTER 12. FOR MY HIGH SCHOOL FRIENDS 133

CHAPTER 13. FOR MY COLLEGE FRIENDS 143

CHAPTER 14. HOW TO BE A SUPPORTER 151

APPENDIX 161

ACKNOWLEDGMENTS 167

INTRODUCTION

Shannon Mason knew she had to start somewhere. The Alaskan native didn't quite know what it would look like once she did, but she knew if she wanted to make it, she'd have to put herself out into the world. So, she packed up her life and moved to New York City.

Think about a time you dared to put yourself out there like that. What did it feel like? Moments like these can be scary, nerve-racking, or confusing when we don't know the outcome. As young women in journalism, putting ourselves out there is a job requirement. When we wake up in the mornings, we decide whether to accept any unpleasant feelings as part of the day's work or to build up our self-confidence and trust in our ability to manage the outcome. Either way, we get out of bed in the mornings and put ourselves out there all over again. In this book, we will discover the passion lying within us to get us to that moment. I want all of us to have a memory we can share in our lives about a time we chose to bet on ourselves, just like Shannon did.

Growing up, Shannon had a dream to work as an intern at *Rolling Stone* magazine. In 2019, she landed that role as a college student. LinkedIn or on internships.com didn't have application links that got her the job. Shannon took the initiative to reach out and introduce herself to an editor at *Rolling Stone*. *Talk about betting on yourself.*

What happened when Shannon requested an informational interview? The editor granted the request. This set in motion a chain of events that ultimately led to her dream journalism internship at *Rolling Stone* magazine. Like any good story, so much more led to up to the moment Shannon received her internship, but we will have to wait a little bit longer to unpack her journey. What I want to focus on right now is her unique and empowered path. As a fellow journalism student at The King's College in New York City, watching a young woman take control of her life in such a confident way has been inspiring. This led me to ask: is this something others are doing? Are they breaking down the traditional route to success in the journalism industry? That seems to be the case. Alternative routes are emerging for journalists, and together, we will discover some of the ways they are happening.

When I say "alternative," all I mean is different. Previously, most people assumed they had to follow a traditional path toward success in the industry: find an interest, study journalism in college, graduate with a degree, and get an entry-level job. Now, thanks to modern technology, we can start building up our careers whenever we want. We can launch a blog, create a YouTube channel, or begin a freelance writing career, all from our phones. Building a following and expanding our skills through these different platforms can open a door into the journalism and media industry,

The way into the industry is not defined by one route—the paths are modern and unique in their own way. The rules of the game are changing, and people are pioneering a new wave of what it means to be a journalist in the twenty-first century.

I've observed this firsthand. I met a former photographer who blazed a trail into publishing her own magazine. I worked at a digital media site cofounded by someone who spent years in the ministry and nonprofit realm. I have even taken classes with young women building up their resumes while balancing school and personal lives. Their stories inspired me, and I can't wait to share them with you.

Not everyone has the same journey. Some start earlier than others, and some get so tired of waiting for someone else to give them a chance that they create their own. The path toward success in the industry can be unique to each and every one of us. I would even go as far as to say I don't *want* all of us to follow the path expected. Let's take a stand together and say that we will not follow anyone else's path. We will be ourselves, get our shovel, and dig our own way to success.

I was compelled to research and write this book because of the people that have surrounded me in my own life—hardworking and passionate women. They have the drive to work hard and create things that shine a light on others. They are college students, CEOs, founders, publishers, and editors. If you wonder how a young journalist with a little more than a couple of fancy-sounding internships to pad my resume can write a book, then I have an answer for you. I set a goal, did the research, made some connections, and jumped at the opportunity.

Every day, I wake up with the mindset of learning something new and searching for ways to grow as a journalist or as an overall human being. As it turns out, many of the women featured in this book have a growth mindset, too. If we focus on keeping ourselves humble to learning new things every day, opportunities will jump up left and right to take us in new directions.

Imagine how excited you were for every new dream you had throughout your childhood. These dreams were unique to us. We had no limitations on what we wanted out of our lives—the possibilities were endless. I want us to use that same energy from when we were kids to create a path for our goals today. Leave behind any negative energy from the past and make a decision to start a new journey today. Everyone's starting point will look different, but I don't want that to deter you from starting in the first place. Focus on the finish line rather than the starting line. This is a pathway that will be carved out special to each and every one of us. Even in my career so far, I have already noticed the path I am going down is unique to me.

One of my first opportunities to have my work published in a magazine was when I was an editorial intern at *D Magazine* in Dallas. The first story assigned to me was about pickleball. Our editor saw a piece done about the sport in a magazine from up north, and he wanted us to do a story about the pickleball culture in Dallas. Since everyone else was busy, they decided to give it to an intern. *Insert me.* First thing I did: Googled "what is pickleball?" *I honestly knew nothing about the topic.* I did extensive research about the Dallas-Fort Worth pickleball culture and interviewed a lovely woman in charge of a local tournament. The piece underwent several edits before it appeared in the August issue, but I was proud of myself for turning an assignment into a fun article.

For a period of my childhood, I dreamed of being a fashion journalist someday. Pickleball wasn't my first choice for a story, but I did what had to be done. In the magazine issue, the pickleball story happened to be placed next to an ad for the Dior exhibit at the Dallas Museum of Art. This was a defining moment internally. It was a sign that if I kept working hard, I would eventually be writing about the things that excite me the most, like the Dior exhibit. I could be covering the newest exhibition at the Dallas Museum of Art one day, or if we dream even bigger, the latest Met Gala collection at the Metropolitan Museum of Art in New York City.

Nothing compares to working hard and seeing your dedication come to life through your work. For me, nothing compares to the process of crafting a pitch, doing the research, spending hours trying to find the right words for an article and reworking them multiple times. In the end, it all feels worth it. This is the beauty of creating our own individual journeys to success, and we don't do it alone. We are surrounded by others along the way, helping us grow and expand our knowledge.

Many of the students, mentors, and managers featured in this book have inspired me to write the words you are reading. Why them specifically? My goal was to hear from people who are just like us: figuring life out one step at a time. They each made their way through the door of the journalism and media industry in one way or another. They each have a unique passion for telling other people's stories.

I discovered my passion for sharing others' stories the summer before my senior year of high school. I had the opportunity to attend the Mayborn Literary Nonfiction Conference through the University of North Texas' Mayborn School of Journalism Multimedia High School Workshop. *Yes, I know that was a mouthful.* The conference theme was "The Power of Words." Students listened to featured speakers and authors, conducted our own research, and interviewed professional journalists about their own work. Being immersed in that environment inspired me as a young, hopeful writer.

A notable name in attendance was Sarah Hepola, author of the best-selling book *Blackout*. Her writings have appeared in the *New York Times Magazine*, *Texas Monthly*, *Elle*, *Bloomberg Businessweek*, *The Guardian*, *Slate*, and *Salon*.[1] I had the chance to interview Sarah about being a published author and experienced journalist, and it was one of the coolest moments as someone who was just getting started. After spending multiple days at the conference, I left wanting to become the best writer I could be and wondering if I could write my own book one day. *(Spoiler alert: here we are three years later).*

The advice I internalized from those professionals has stuck with me. Jeffrey Weiss, a former *Dallas Morning News* writer who has since passed away, told us in an interview, "Do more journalism folks. Do journalism, and make sure it's good journalism." Seems simple, right? Every day I have made a commitment to Weiss, myself, and all the other journalists who have come before me to not let this idea fall through the cracks. Being on a mission to "do good journalism" has fueled my desire to find the truth and report it factually while helping others do the same. Doing good journalism means doing it well and doing it to help others.

Recently, when I announced I was writing this book, a fellow Mayborn workshop student commented on my post, "Remember when we interviewed Sarah together and got to drool over all of the other successful writers at the Mayborn conference?" *Yes, Maddie, I do remember that!* This moment

---

[1] "About The Author," Sarah Hepola, accessed September 6, 2020.

made me realize something. At seventeen years old, I had the chance to interview authors with successful books, and now I am writing a book of my own. Just imagine the possibilities to come for us.

Why are we having these conversations? By the end of this book, we will understand why getting started is the most challenging but most rewarding part of our journeys. Together, we will discover the importance of looking beyond the immediate obstacles in our paths to see the possibilities of what we can do. We will recognize the space available to lay down a foundation for our path based on what we value. We will master what it means to be courageous, curious, confident, and valuable as we start to go after what we want.

This book is for women, and men, looking for some guidance as they begin their careers. We will walk away with essential life lessons.

- We will learn to build a foundational system to work off of, why we should stay dedicated to our values, and discover how to be open to new opportunities.
- We will learn how to pivot at different points in our careers and decide if we need a change.
- We will learn how to inspire others and use the information as guiding tools to be teachers, professors, parents, partners, siblings, and more.

Skillsets are learned, but passion and confidence come from within. We have to bring it out of ourselves. It's time to stop waiting until we have *all* of the skills we think we need and just get started. *Beyond the Title* is for someone with a courageous and curious drive, and you wouldn't be here if that wasn't already within you.

PART ONE

THE INDUSTRY

CHAPTER ONE

WHAT IS JOURNALISM?

My dad begins every morning the same way he always has. When I was a child, he spent most mornings sitting on the brown couch, feet propped up, drinking his coffee (*black with a splash of milk*), and reading the newspaper. Today, my father remains a creature of habit. On any given morning, I can walk into the living room and see him sitting on the same brown couch, feet propped up, drinking his coffee (*black with a splash of milk*). The one thing that *has* changed is that he now scrolls through the news on his phone rather than on newsprint. I didn't appreciate the power of printed words on newsprint when I was younger. But those pages held everything from the local news, national issues, the state of the economy, obituaries, job openings, and so much more. The pages had life within them; life brought to us by journalism.

    Dad always saw in me the makings of a marketing professional while I thought I'd grow up to become a model. It was during my binge-watching of America's Next Top Model as a kid that I realized my five-foot-four height was not going to get me into the doors of the modeling industry. As I entered high school (*a full-fledged adult, obviously*), I figured I needed to find what I was going to do for a career. Until I took a journalism class as an elective as a high school freshman, I hadn't thought much about journalism as a career. After my first semester, it seemed my destiny was to fall in love with journalism. *Sorry, Dad.*

I believe the purpose of journalism is to inform. Information is one of our society's most valuable pieces, and not everyone knows how to access it. There is a relationship between those with resources to acquire information and those who seek to learn from it. We should cover a few basics about the subject before we get started. First, aim for accurate details and always fight to reveal the truth that wants to stay hidden. Second, we must be aware of any biases we may have and disclose this in our work. We cannot escape our biases. Our upbringings and the culture around us form our biases, but bias isn't always a negative thing. There can be value in using biases to create a diverse newsroom and expand our conversations to better serve our audiences.

The American Press Institute, whose goal is to advance an innovative and sustainable news industry, believes the basis of journalism is built on gathering, assessing, creating, and presenting news and information.[2] As I mentioned before, journalism is an art fulfilled by giving information to the public. That is the core of journalism.

When someone enters the journalism profession, they are agreeing to find the truth and share information. I will never sit here and say everyone has the purest intentions, but it is way above my pay grade to decipher what is going on in someone else's head (*therapists exist for that, and bless their*

---

2   "About Us," American Press Institute, Accessed June 9, 2020.

souls for doing what they do). Journalists inform the public by sharing the stories found from around the world, and *we* can utilize different resources to share them.

Someone who utilizes resources well is Kate Adie. Kate filled the chief news correspondent seat on the British Broadcasting Corporation Network for fourteen years (*That's the BBC… Americans may recognize that label from watching reruns of* Doctor Who *every Friday night. Unless that's just me…*). When speaking of her experiences as a war correspondent, she once said, "I keep telling myself to calm down, to take less of an interest in things and not get so excited, but I still care a lot about liberty, freedom of speech, and expression, and the fairness in journalism."[3] Kate touches on what many journalists fight for daily: to protect liberty with fairness and care about what we are reporting on.

Kate has also written five different books. She covers the legacy of women from the First World War in her book *Fighting on the Home Front: The Legacy of Women in World War I*. BBC 2 turned the text into a documentary broadcast to go with the Corporation's WW1 Centenary Season.[4] Most will see the book and the documentary, but I encourage you to see their purpose. Listen, read, and take in the story presented and what she wants to inform us about. As a journalist, Kate gave life to a piece of history that we may not have known about before. She is just one of the women in the journalism world that helped pave the way for the others.

Kate and others can be inspirations for young journalists because of a trial that occurred in 1735. John Zenger was the printer of a publication called *The New York Weekly Journal*

---

3   Luke Bilton, "Kate Adie: 'I Never Desired to Go into War Zones. It Just Sort of Happened as Part of the Job,'" *IFSEC Global*. March 17, 2016.
4   "Books," Katie Adie's Official Website, Accessed June 9, 2020.

and published articles that openly critiqued the local government. Zenger printed the pieces anonymously to protect his writers, but this ultimately led to his arrest in 1733 under a libel accusation. Libel, at the time, was when you published information that opposed the government. Zenger's trial focused on whether he had published the articles—an act he'd never denied—rather than on whether the articles he published contained untruths. Andrew Hamilton defended Zenger, and his defense tactic was simple: he admitted that Zenger did print the papers. He wanted to appeal to the jury's thoughts and feelings about freedom. Hamilton wanted the jury to fight for Zenger's release for "the cause of liberty."[5]

The jury's only job was to decide if they believed that Zenger printed the stories. They had the choice either to send a man to jail or to protect the liberty of the people and set him free. In the end, jury members decided Zenger was not guilty of libel. They saved him from imprisonment for sharing the truth by agreeing that he did not publish the stories.[6]

The Zenger trial is a building block of liberty and the press's freedom and is still taught to journalists today. If you are ever on Wall Street in Manhattan, keep an eye out for a big, old building called Federal Hall. The building stands on the same spot where the Zenger trial happened all those years ago. I had the opportunity to sit on the Federal Hall steps for my Media Law and Ethics class. We sat on the steps and discussed how the trial affects our roles today as journalists, and how far the industry has come since that trial. It was a moment for us to embrace the freedom of speech and the value of a free press.

---
5   "The Trial of John Peter Zenger," USHistory.org, Accessed September 30, 2020.
6   Ibid.

"It is not the cause of one poor printer," Hamilton claimed, "but the cause of liberty."[7]

The trial of John Zenger helped pave a passage to the first amendment we know and love today. We can now publish the truth without fear of punishment. We get to embrace the press' freedom that Zenger and Hamilton helped set a path for and build upon their foundational trial. Every person has a story to share, and journalists are looking for these stories, whether they are happy, sad, infuriating, or inspiring. When we report on an earthquake, we report on the damage it caused and share the news worldwide. We report on the local high school football game because not everyone can attend but still wants to support it.

Throughout this book, we will dive deep into the lives of people who have created their careers from the purpose of informing and sharing stories. Whether it's a magazine or online digital media site, they are looking to inform because that *is* the basis of journalism. If you want to pursue a journalism industry career or support someone who does, then build a foundation with that principle. Once we understand the purpose of journalism, our creativity and drive will take us to new heights.

---

7   Ibid.

CHAPTER TWO

MULTI-MEDIA JOURNALISM

―――

If we are playing a spitfire questionnaire game and you ask me on the spot if I prefer print or online journalism, then I would answer you quickly. I am a lover of print journalism, and more specifically, I have a deep passion for magazine journalism.

The magazines at the end of the checkout lanes at the grocery store caught my attention at a young age. Their placement next to the candy may have been a contributing factor, but I couldn't help wanting to learn more about the stories behind the glossy covers. As a teenager, I wondered what it would be like to work for one of my favorite magazines. But it was always a lofty "what if" dream.

If not for a pivotal conversation with my high school guidance counselor, Laura Phillips, I might have spent the rest of my life stuck in a "what if" mindset. When I met with Mrs. Phillips my senior year, I told her all about an exciting scholarship I had found for a school in New York. The catch was that I would have to ask my parents to let me travel from

Texas to New York City to compete in the competition, and I was *terrified*. I wasn't afraid they'd get upset or anything; I was afraid they'd say no.

Mrs. Phillips waited for a pause in the discussion as I tried to talk myself out of even trying. Then she asked, "Do you really want to spend the rest of your life wondering what could have been?"

I thought about the guidance counselor's question all the way home. *Did I want to spend the rest of my life wondering what could have been?*

That afternoon, I sat down with my parents—who had never even stepped foot in New York City, at that point—I took a deep breath and popped the big question. To my surprise, they immediately said yes. They're not the spontaneous type, but dad grabbed his laptop and booked a flight right away. *Thank you, Southwest Airlines, for coming through with those cheap flights.*

My dad and I flew out on a 6:00 a.m. flight to New York City on a chilly November day and arrived in the concrete jungle, running on very little sleep. We were in the city for one reason only: get in, compete, and get out. I had twenty-four hours to try and win a full-ride scholarship. The competition question: what would be your dream internship in the city? My choice: *Marie Claire*.

Marie Claire magazine produces content that connects with women. I feel inspired by its feature stories and lifestyle articles. In the end, I didn't win the scholarship competition, but my passion for magazines and for *Marie Claire* remained undiminished. *Marie Claire, you can give me a call anytime.*

A passion for telling stories and sharing them brings together journalists of all types. Words are the foundation of journalism, and we use the power behind them to tell compelling stories. The process of writing goes beyond stringing syllables together to make coherent, *or what we hope are coherent*, sentences for an article that will engage readers.

What do we learn in the writing process? We learn how to convey emotions through descriptions, visuals, and language. The goal is not to "tell" our audience how they should feel, but rather create an atmosphere where they can decide on their own. We have a responsibility to effectively create a narrative that empowers our audiences to decide for themselves how they perceive the story without any direct influence.

We can incorporate the writing process when brainstorming how to effectively share a story for higher audience engagement rates. There needs to be a connection between the creator and the consumer, and ample opportunities to achieve that will occur once we learn how to identify stories around us. Prioritize the ideal consumer. Consider the audience you **want** to engage with your content but also consider the audience who **will** engage with your content. The audience you will be linking with will dictate how much impact a story will have, so it's vital to make it worth their time.

Journalists are not merely writers. They are producers, broadcasters, podcasters, and radio hosts as well. In 2020, journalists can use social media as a storytelling platform. YouTube, Instagram, Facebook, Twitter, and even TikTok offer direct routes between journalists and consumers. The journalistic purpose remains the same: to inform and share stories.

Using the writing process on different platforms helps script out the best ways to convey stories. Limitations, for example, will restrict how long a tweet can be, the length of an Instagram story, or what music can be used in the background of a YouTube video. Despite these factors, the potential for creativity is waiting to burst out and on our screens.

We can grow a loyal audience through different aesthetics and productions, and when something unique to you catches people's attention, run with it. Trends are consistently changing and fading, and we want to be on the right side of it (*psst... you can also get ahead by being creative and starting your own trends*).

One word or image can change the tone of a story completely and cause potential long-term damage to a brand. Using the writing process is paramount in every type of production. People have instant access to whatever we post and the ability to share everything posted, whether it is good or bad.

Anita Li understands how dynamic digital mediums can be. A former editor at *Mashable*, Li founded *The Other Wave*, a website that explores film and television from a diverse perspective. In her 2015 TED Talk, "The Power of Digital Journalism," Li explained she'd wanted the site to have a strong focus on navigating the evolution of digital journalism. She saw an opportunity to brainstorm ways to cover the news creatively and be influential on the Internet.[8]

In her talk, Li described having grown up reading and watching the news as a fourth meal of the day (*I think Li and my Dad may have this in common*). Bold newspaper headlines and the people on television were practically her childhood friends. As a budding journalist, she looked beyond the news production to see the reporters. The journalists that filled Li's daily routine as a child represent a gold standard of news for her: fast, accurate, and reliable.[9]

---

8   *TEDx Talks*, "The Power of Digital Journalism | Anita Li | TEDxDistilleryDistrictWomen," August 5, 2015, video, 8:42.
9   *TEDx Talks*, "The Power of Digital Journalism."

"They loomed large in my mind as I worked towards my lifelong goal of becoming a professional storyteller," Li reflected in her talk. "When I finally got to join Canada's storied institutions and I reported for several, I felt a deep sense of achievement."[10]

Journalists like Li have been using the writing process to tell stories for a long time and are consistently looking for ways to upgrade the way we share it. How can we keep improving our way of describing, visualizing, and telling a story? Journalists aspire to become the reporters they watched, read, and listened to growing up. It's a constant cycle of inspiration. There is beauty in this evolving circle; dreamers become students, and students become teachers. The way we tell stories may change, but the power of the stories will not.

New journalists are entering an industry constantly evolving the way we share stories in three different categories: digital media, print, and blogging.

Digital Media

Online media requires a constant flow of articles and uploads, and breaking the first story can be a fight. News outlets continually battle each other to be the first one to break any news and be the first one with an article published. Why is that? They are fighting for viewership and site clicks. Breaking news articles in this fast-paced environment will most likely have a few sentences and a note stating it will be updated as the event unfolds. The first outlet to break a story has an advantage for audience engagement.

---

10   *TEDx Talks*, "The Power of Digital Journalism."

This is the nature of online media. We can get things up as soon as possible, make additions as we go, and fix corrections as needed. People have instant access to our content that they can share it as they see fit, which increases audience engagement through social media. One article can start a conversation on Twitter, a post on Instagram can increase followers, and Facebook posts can lead to clicking a link to a site. This is the ultimate goal when it comes to advertisement revenue and memberships to bring in money to a media company. Companies wishing to advertise their product on a digital media site are looking for high viewership and engagement before investing their own marketing dollars. Digital media can track site analytics and social media engagement to propose rates to advertisers.

Instant access through a two-way delivery system means that when we get it right, we go viral and we immediately know we nailed it. And when we get it wrong—well, we still go viral, and Twitter very well may blow up and implode on us. Digital news has a level of responsibility to produce product quickly but without sacrificing accuracy and reliability. Once we put our content out into the digital space, there's no retracting an error. We can delete an error, sure, but nothing on the Internet is truly temporary. Now more than ever, we only get one chance to get it right.

Digital media is not going to disappear any time soon. This leaves journalists facing three different challenges: how to produce accurate reporting as quickly as possible, how to distribute content to a large sector of people, and how to monetize a digital product. It is important to remember where the money goes when complaining about paying for online journalism. The small amount of money you pay to go behind the firewall of a news site funds the salaries of the journalists who work to keep a community informed. The evolution of digital media has just begun, and you might even be the innovator who reimagines the future of digital journalism.

Print

My ideal, rainy Saturday morning begins with a hot latte and a trip to Half Price Books. I love to dig through their magazine section. People drop off new and old magazines all the time, and it's the best way to build up a collection on a budget. *Especially when they are being sold again for one dollar.* I have at least a hundred magazines buried under my childhood bed in Texas. The dream is to have a massive magazine showcase in my home one day, but until then, I'll continue to hoard them.

My attraction to the print medium has a lot to do with the delicate process of creating a magazine; from the meetings to plan out every page within each section to the research, writing, editing and fact-checking of each piece. Before it hits the paper, the team will design a layout with graphics or photos to create the final product. There is just something special about that type of print journalism.

This same kind of energy is within different print mediums. There is no room for error with newspapers, magazines, and nonfiction books. Errors are difficult to fix when they're already printed and can damage reputations. Mistakes are costly to fix when they're caught and perhaps even more costly when they're not. *Like I said, a very delicate process.*

Fact-checking is an intense but a very vital piece in the print journalism process. My mind would be worn out after fact-checking feature pieces as an intern for *D Magazine*. It's what I spent majority of my time doing. No one purposely makes errors, but they do happen. Catching them is paramount.

Our fact-checking process began with the piece being printed out on a piece of paper. We highlighted every name of a person, place, and thing to double-check the spelling letter by letter. Then, we would highlight the facts and double-check them with sources. I once fact-checked Dirk Nowitzki's name for an article, and that meant crossing through every letter of every single one of the fifty Dirk's on the paper. We highlighted any questionable piece of information because it's always better to be safe than sorry.

Print journalism has slowly faded in places due to a lack of budgeting, but its delicacy will never go away. The industry is finding ways to keep it alive and thriving, and the little girl within me is appreciative of that. I want to hold your work in my hands, and I want to get wrapped up in the world without a notification interrupting me. It's time to get back to basics in the storytelling world.

Blog

The growth of digital media has played a role in growing the blogging and influencer sector of the internet. Blogging has become a powerful industry, but there are clear distinctions between bloggers and journalists. Both research, write, edit, and publish, but sometimes blogs are not factually accurate.

We have to be careful about the "news" we intake from blogs. When they back it up with reporting and research, or link to someone who does, then that is something we can work with. People can easily claim to be journalists on the Internet, and readers don't know their true intentions.

Lifestyle bloggers who are just sharing personal stories and thoughts are a different scenario. This is something digital media has empowered. It is giving platforms to the people who didn't feel like they had one before. We can share our stories with the world today with a simple click of a button. *That fact slightly terrifies me.* We cannot deny the power in that, good and bad. I encourage everyone to filter what they are reading online and decide to raise up the voices of those looking to spread goodness.

Blogs can make money from advertisement revenues and sponsorships. There is a lot of money within the sponsorships realm of the Internet. The key here is audience engagement and understanding what your viewers want to see, very similar to how journalists have to think when posting content online.

Blogs are a great opportunity to develop our writing skills and become better storytellers. Blogging can be a side hustle as someone builds up a journalistic resume, and if that interests you, then go for it. It can be a supplement to your professional work when done correctly. One thing I do *not* want you to get into the habit of as a blogger, journalist, and overall writer is the clickbait trend. *That's right—I want you to say it with me.*

"I will not become a clickbait writer to gain more views and engagement."

If the word clickbait makes you cringe right away, this is a good thing. Clickbait is "something (such as a headline) designed to make readers want to click on a hyperlink especially when the link leads to content of dubious value or interest."¹¹ Journalists should not be entertaining clickbait or participating in it. The practice is not a credible way to boost our audiences, gain attention, or increase viewership. If we stay true to the underlying purpose of why we are working hard to produce good journalism, then it will pay off in the end.

Digital, print, and blogs interact all together in different ways. Print articles can be posted online, turned into a conversation on social media, and made into a YouTube video. Then, blogs can turn around and reference it in their own post. Overall, engagement can be increased with all three integrated. Journalists are expected to be able to write, record videos, and do more as multi-media journalists since the online world has taken the forefront.

Whether we are working in digital, print, or for a blog, we must remember why we do what we do. Journalism is about informing and telling stories (*and I'll keep saying it until it's tattooed in our heads*). With that as a purpose, the possibilities of influence and empowerment are endless.

---

11   *Merriam-Webster.com Dictionary*, s.v. "clickbait," accessed August 22, 2020.

CHAPTER THREE

FINDING A FIELD OF VISION

Let's set a scene, shall we? Imagine a butterfly. A multicolored butterfly who has expanded its wings and is flying around without a care in the world. Taking in all the sights in its field of vision and trying to navigate the next adventure. There is a mixture of colors in the daylight as it flies through all the nature around us. This butterfly has waited for its freedom to dance in the sun and explore the city ahead.

Now, let's add some background. Picture the Brooklyn Bridge beaming over the East River separating the boroughs of Manhattan and Brooklyn. There is a stillness to the water, but it's a whole new world to explore for the butterfly. The insect has taken off and is ready to explore the land in front of them. Not even the rustic brown of the bridge and surrounding buildings can dull out the butterfly.

I like to consider my story to be similar to the butterfly's. The Seaport District at Pier 17 is one of my favorite spots in the city, and many fond memories of the Brooklyn Bridge are sketched into my head. Just a young journalist trying my best to be a brave woman exploring the opportunities around her. Some of my childhood friends swear my life is like a Hallmark movie: a small-town girl chases her dreams to New York City. I quickly dismiss this as not being accurate when it is said to me, but I'll let you make your verdict (*and if there are any producers ever reading this, I have a few options to play this "Lauren" character... just throwing that out there*).

Rewind to 2013, five years before I moved to New York City. I loved to read but never dreamed I'd write a book of my own someday. I had, however, begun to flirt with the idea of becoming a writer. In eighth grade, we had to do a research assignment on the topic of our choice. It was the time of the "More Issues Than Vogue" phone case trend, which inspired my choice of Vogue editor Anna Wintour as my research subject. The essay highlighted my initial interest in the journalism and publication world. After the project, two things were apparent: people fascinate me, and I easily get lost in their stories.

The people we look up to in our lives can teach us to make practical life decisions, if we choose those people wisely. The "dreaming is nice, but be practical" conversation makes part of our childhood disappear. Our goals are gradually aimed at a path that is sustainable, rather than something that ignites the fire of passion within. Knowing my passion, I searched for a path that would be an investment in future but would still excite my inner child.

That little journalism class I landed in as a high school freshman fueled a new passion. My first assignment for class was to write about the Charlie Hebdo attacks in Paris, France, in 2015. It was during my early draft check-in that my teacher looked at me and said, "Lauren, this is really good." That moment helped grow the nagging inside me that I had indeed found something I could do and *love* doing for the rest of my life. Mrs. Kidder, *if you stumble across this, thank you for that.*

Just before I entered my senior year, I attended the University of North Texas Mayborn School of Journalism High School Workshop. Recently, I stumbled across a short answer I used for my application to the program. It said:

> "I want to attend the workshop because I know how much growing I need to do, how much learning I have to do, and I want to dive into the potential I know I have. I want to study journalism in college. I would love to live and work in either New York or London. I believe there is a calling for young journalists right now in our world. We need to have more journalists fighting to find the truth in the news and share it with the world. I want to be a part of the new generation of journalists."

This is what we are learning to do: become better journalists and be the leaders of the next generation. This focus is what lead me to move away from home in August 2018. I packed up way too many things into several suitcases and moved to New York City. That was only the beginning of my journey.

Iridescent Women

As a college freshman, I eagerly attended my school's internship fair, determined to find a way to prove myself and grow my skills. Immediately, I was—you might say—distracted by the shiny object in the room. *Iridescent Women*, a digital media site, caught my eye with their bright and colorful display amongst the other dull and muted tables. I couldn't help but want to find out more information on the company.

Iridescent Women is a vibrant group of women that encourages others to share their stories in an authentic way to connect with, help, and inspire the community around us. That's what attracted me to them.

My application was a simple email stuffed with my high school resume and my hopes that my little high school experience would be enough. And it was just enough to land me an interview with *Iridescent Women* cofounder Nicole Smithee. I hustled and bustled my way through New York City streets for my first interview with Nicole. My caramel brown palooza pants, "Future is Female" t-shirt, and big backpack did not scream, "I just moved here from the south!" A fire grew within me that day to prove that I did have my place in the city next to the other young professionals.

Nicole and I met at The Wing in NYC's SoHo neighborhood. The Wing is a space with communal tables and working stations for women, but they also host events for mingling and networking opportunities for members. The building was not attractive outside, but it was one of the most vibrant places I have ever been to. On The Wing's floor, women were everywhere—some chatting, many typing away on laptops—and the whole area screamed modern-retro glamour. *All I could think was, "this is why I moved to New York."* Nicole and I chatted about our shared love for women empowerment, and at that moment, I felt in my heart that I needed to work for Nicole.

My year-long internship with *Iridescent Women* focused on learning new skills and finding a community of women who were authentically honest in everything they do. As a writing intern, I would visit Nicole most Friday afternoons after class to work with her one-on-one. We would always meet at The Wing's location in Dumbo, Brooklyn. Between the waterfront's calm waves and the view of Manhattan, the small area became my weekly sanctuary. I would spend time on the benches by the water and reflect on everything going on. It was in those moments that I allowed myself to be proud of how far I had come and to dream of where I could go.

My work with Nicole fell under an umbrella of tasks, from uploading articles to the website, picking out header photos, sending contributor emails, helping plan out the content schedule, and working for social media. Seeing what goes on behind the scenes of a digital media site is how I fell in love with the branding, communications, and content creation.

Nicole became a mentor to me during the time we spent together. Her kind words and advice were always so warming, and she is even one of my featured people in this book. *The gift that keeps on giving,* is what I like to say. As my first internship role, *Iridescent Women* created the foundation for my skills. Dipping my toe into multiple sections of the site helped set me up for my next internship.

This is the beauty of our first internships. We go in having no idea what to expect but leave knowing where we would like to take our next step.

D Magazine

My uncle Milton had been diagnosed with cancer right before I moved fifteen hundred miles away from home. Home became a simple, but seemingly long, three-and-a-half-hour plane ride away. I have a small family. It's a tiny bunch that can crack me up at any moment and probably needs to come with a warning label before interacting with them. Family is my backbone and the reason why I do what I do.

What I am about to say may sound quirky, but hear me out and re-read the statement before you put the book down. My mother's sister married my dad's brother (*never gets old, saying that*). My mom, Teresa, only has one sister, Debra. My dad, Joe, had two brothers, Rick and Milton, and two sisters, Ginger and Rose. My aunt Debra and uncle Rick eventually got together along with my parents. Here we are all these years later, weird to some, but perfect to me. Somebody mentioned one time that it's funny to think that your cousins have cousins that you don't know. This is not the case for me. I have a small number of cousins, and we all know each other pretty well.

My freshman year, on a morning I was set to fly back to the city after being home for the holidays, we got a phone call that my uncle was in the hospital and we needed to get there urgently. I don't remember many tedious memories vividly, but that day may be engraved in my memory forever. I started crying instantly that dreadful morning as I sat on our couch, suitcase in hand and ready to go to the airport. It hit me that I wasn't going to get to say goodbye.

Somehow life has an extraordinary way of having beautiful moments within distressing times. A notification five minutes later revealed my flight's cancellation that day—no delay, just canceled with no reasoning. I rebooked my flight for the afternoon and put my stuff in the car so that we could go to the hospital. That one canceled flight is a moment I will oddly be forever grateful for happening. My extra hours that day to were used to say goodbye to my uncle and for one last chance to hear him say, "be careful up there." Then, I got on a plane and flew back to the city that held my dreams in its hands—gripping to me even in a time of agony.

Just when March started to bloom that same semester, I received another grim phone call that my grandmother was in the hospital. My grandma had Alzheimer's for as long as I could remember, and her health had deteriorated throughout my teenage years. She passed away the day after my nineteenth birthday, and the stories people share about her make me wish I would have known her in her prime. Part of me likes to think my granny would be proud of how far I have come. My aunt and uncle found an old photo from when she was younger, and we discovered that I am practically her doppelgänger (*for the most part*), with the same cheekbones and smile. She was a strong woman who had a direct impact on me being where I am today.

With the gloomy semester on my mind, I still found the motivation to apply for a *D Magazine* summer internship. I felt like I owed it to myself to honor the people taken from me too soon. The time had come to move forward and continue to do better for them and me. I had my eyes set on a summer internship going into my freshman year, and after spending my first semester thriving with *Iridescent Women*, I felt like I was ready.

D Magazine tackles all things lifestyle, food, culture, life, and more within the Dallas area. As a *D Magazine* intern, I did a lot of fact-checking, wrote articles, and would help with miscellaneous things here and there. I worked under Christiana Nielson, the former managing editor for *D Magazine*. Working with Christiana was precisely what I needed; she was direct, supportive, and very organized.

It could have been the free coffee in the office that made me love the internship, but really, I learned so much from fellow interns and the newsroom. I dealt with many different sources, worked on my communication skills, and developed my professionalism. That summer, I attended events like Taste of Dallas and became more immersed in the North Texas culture. When it came to writing, god bless Christiana, because my writing was a little rough at the time. She knew how to edit, and I embraced everything she said. She taught me how to tell a story within each sentence of a piece and to be engaging with my writing.

What I walked away from *D Magazine* with was the understanding that I can be as successful as I allow myself to be. I had the ideas for stories, but my fear of rejection got in the way of me pitching them. Two of my published articles were ones I pitched as online pieces, but it was Christiana's idea to pitch them for the print issue. She is the one who encouraged me to turn the stories' potential into tangible pieces.

If we are standing in the way of our potential, then we don't see what others see in us. *D Magazine* was a pivotal point in me figuring this out about myself. Journalists have to be confident in their skills and be courageous in how they put themselves out there. We have to believe in what we can do. Imagine if the journalists before who broke massive stories decided not to take the first step to write them? Now, we have the chance to be the ones creating those stories.

Iridescent Women and *D Magazine* had an emotional impact on me as well. These experiences were steps in my journey toward writing this book today. And writing this book is a step in my journey toward whatever lies ahead. The women featured in this book continue through theirs, and it's time for you to join us. It's time to be like the butterfly in an exciting new area, dancing in the sun and exploring what lies ahead.

PART TWO

THE FOUNDATIONS

CHAPTER FOUR

YOU HAVE TO START SOMEWHERE

What would you say is the hardest part of driving a car? Is it starting it? Or driving it?

Unlocking a door, inserting a key, and turning it to start up an engine is the first step to driving. We cannot do anything without starting it first. If we want to go on a short journey or extended road trip, nothing can happen until we start the car. We cannot begin on the path to an endpoint if we don't have our transportation. You are probably sitting there going, "Well, yeah? That's how a car works, Lauren."

Take a moment to compare your goals to that road trip in your car. If you don't grab the keys and open the door, nothing will happen. If you don't start the car, nothing will happen. If we don't grab hold of the resources available around us, then we may not be open to new opportunities to start somewhere. We have to start the engine and drive along the road to our future.

In 2009, three Harvard undergrads started their metaphorical car to launch a website called Her Campus. Stephanie

Kaplan Lewis, Annie Wang, and Windsor Hanger Western met while working for a student-run women's publication on campus. The publication quickly gained popularity at Harvard, and soon students across the nation wanted to know how they could replicate it for their own campuses. Instead, Stephanie, Annie, and Windsor decided to build a national publication to serve college women everywhere. They entered, and won, the 2009 Harvard business plan competition with their vision for Her Campus Media and launched their company as college students with financial assistance from winning. The company has become a starting point for young journalists, writers, and creators around the world. Over the years, Her Campus Media expanded to include Spoon University, College Fashionista, and the InfluenceHer Collective. They remain 100 percent women-owned-and-operated.[12]

What was going through their minds as college students in 2009? The women felt that there was a hole to fill in the media market. They set out to create "an online magazine dedicated to, written by, and focused on empowering, college women."[13] The site itself hosts college journalists from all over the world. The InfluencerHer Collective has four thousand millennial influencers; they created the Her Conference, a College Fashion Week, a High School Ambassador Program, Campus Trendsetters, the Her Campus Shop, and a book called *The Her Campus Guide to College Life*. Her Campus's reach is undeniable, with over 360 chapters at college campuses across eleven countries.[14]

---

12 "About," Her Campus Media, accessed June 19, 2020.
13 "About Us," Her Campus, accessed June 19, 2020.
14 Ibid.

Stephanie, Annie, and Windsor chose to start somewhere and see where they could go with their idea. Sometimes, getting started is the hardest part of the journey.

Shannon Mason got a head start on her journey. At the age of seven, Shannon interviewed her neighbors about a stray cat. "Have you seen this cat? Do you know who it belongs to?" Shannon wrote down the facts she thought were important in her investigation about the mysterious cat in her neighborhood. Shannon knew she wanted to write from a young age, and her journey to discover the cat owner was the beginning of her journalistic development. Her next step toward journalism began with writing for some local papers before going to college, but at the time, she wasn't really trained in writing a journalistic story. She knew she had to start somewhere as a young adult but didn't exactly know where.

Shannon knew that attending a college with a journalism program was vital for her. Specifically, she wanted to major in journalism through a certified program, and not just a minor, to ensure she got the best journalistic education. She felt naïve about the college search process as neither of her parents went to college. The lack of journalism programs and majors were a significant hiccup in her search process. Some colleges may suggest majoring in English or communications and minoring in journalism. Pursuing journalism as a major was make or break for Shannon. She went into the college search process thinking, "I want a journalism major. I don't want a journalism minor. I don't want to major in English. I want to major in journalism."

Her passion for journalism led the Alaskan native to tour The King's College (TKC), a small Christian liberal arts school in the Financial District of New York City. *(Sound familiar? Shannon and I met through school).* She initially liked King's, but the lack of an official journalism major kept her from fully committing. In a surprise turn of events, a counselor pulled Shannon aside on one of her initial visits to King's to inform her of a new program being announced for the next school year: Journalism, Culture, and Society (JCS).

"I was really excited to be part of something that's just becoming something," Shannon said. "I get a lot of input. I get to shape this experience how I want it to be."

Shannon moved to New York City and began her journey in August of 2017. She published her first article for the school newspaper website, the *Empire State Tribune (EST)*, that October. Campus newspapers at larger universities often require students to have completed prerequisite classes. King's students can take the leap into writing as freshmen with guidance from faculty advisors and the section editors.

Thanks to her early start, when Sharon graduates in December 2020, her resume highlights will already include experiences as the social media editor, managing editor, and editor-in-chief for the *EST* at King's. Her most recent roles were with *Rolling Stone Magazine* and Twisted Valley Farms.

I have had the joy of learning from Shannon as a fellow student, but also as a friend. Now you can learn from her, too. Through her insights and advice, we'll learn to see the value of small internships and school newspapers when it comes to gaining real-world experience before graduation day.

The Potential of Your First Job

People advised Shannon to avoid applying for internships or jobs during her first semester when she arrived in the city so that she wouldn't overwhelm herself. She listened to this and decided to start writing for the school paper, the *Empire State Tribune (EST)*, instead. The *EST* had a lot of potential for new students to make their mark on the paper. It felt like God was guiding her in the direction of journalism and the school paper that year.

The newest *EST* editor-in-chief at the time, Bernadette, sat next to her in Introduction to Journalism. Bernadette had taken classes out of order and ended up making a connection with the freshman. The newly elected EIC encouraged Shannon to go out for being an editor her sophomore year. The paper is composed of an editor-in-chief overseeing a small editorial team. The editorial team comprises micro-editors for different sections of the newspaper: sports editor, city editor, culture editor, opinion editor, and more. They help find new articles and edit pieces before sending them to the editor-in-chief and managing editor.

Shannon hadn't even considered applying for any editor positions for her sophomore year, but they introduced a new one: the social media editor. She ended up applying for the job and became the inaugural social media editor. Shannon spent her summer doing a lot of branding for the school paper and developing their social media presence. She remembers picking out colors and photos and helping redo the website. The plot twist here? Shannon very much disliked her job.

"It was the worst thing I've ever done in my life because it was so not who I am," Shannon reflected. "I [don't] feel like I can artificially put something out there and speak on behalf of a brand. That is so not my thing."

Before long, Shannon figured out which aspects of the social media editor role she disliked. There is always going to be a chance that we end up doing something we don't prefer. Shannon went through the first semester of her sophomore year hating—I mean, *doing*—her job and stumbled upon an opportunity. The former managing editor quit her role going into the spring semester. *Life has a weird way of working out, huh?*

The managing editor is the right hand of the editor-in-chief and spends a lot of time editing articles and posting content on the website. Suddenly, the position was available and up for grabs. A golden opportunity presented itself for Shannon to find a new role within the newspaper team. After speaking with Bernadette, she deemed the managing editor position as something Shannon would enjoy more than social media. Ready for something new, and for an opportunity to learn more, Shannon strutted right into her new role as the *EST* managing editor for the remaining part of the school year.

This is the beauty of your first job. You may not like every aspect of it, but it is worth it. Everyone has to start somewhere, and no matter what kind of role you take on, it's a step toward your future. Shannon took a chance on being a social media editor, and while she didn't thoroughly enjoy it, she put her best foot forward. Then, it opened a door for her. She believes if she hadn't taken a chance on the social media editor role, then the managing editor position would not have been offered. And she would not have been editor-in-chief the next year if she hadn't taken a leap in the dark on being the social media editor.

"Do everything," Shannon said. "If you get a role for something that you really don't want to do, just do it. Get the experience. You can go pretty far with just doing something for a little while that you might not like. There could be the day where they're like, 'We need someone to write this thing right now. Can you write it?' And you'd be like, 'I can write it.' Because you're there, and you're someone who can do it."

First jobs will appear everywhere; we just have to gamble on what we can learn from them. If you are lucky to have a school newspaper on campus, it's a great starting point.

What You Can Learn from a School Paper

Shannon worked as the social media editor, managing editor, and editor-in-chief of the *Empire State Tribune* during her time at The King's College. Being involved with the paper helped her expand her writing and editing skills, but she also gained personal management skills and developed her mindset.

Shannon's major shift from social media to editing opened the door to find out the backend of how everything operated. Her roles helped her see a new field of vision altogether. She slowly learned what makes an article stand out and spent hours assisting students in rewriting articles and teaching others where to begin. She dedicated time to expanding her own knowledge and skills through the experience as well. The consistent correcting of others' grammar, AP style, and language helped mature her skills, reflected in her own writing.

Former editors also laid down a solid foundation for Shannon to build on during her time as EIC, and she sought to do the same with her moment in the role. She spent time brainstorming how to grow the *Empire State Tribune*, and Shannon went to work. This meant creating new podcast episodes, making the print magazine incredibly attractive, and adding things to make the website's content reach new levels. The expansion brought out a new side of her: her business management and innovation skills.

"I think, like, editors-in-chief are so much more business-oriented than people think initially," Shannon stated. "I'm always trying to think about ways that we could be doing better things. You have to really think ahead. You really have to think about years ahead, and I think that is very innovative thinking. You have to be always onto the next thing."

Shannon knows the changes she enacted during her time as EIC may not be seen while she is a student at TKC. She based her strategy on the idea of sustainability. She wanted to create something that could be left beyond her time at the paper. Her legacy also included the staff she managed and how their roles developed over the year. The way she led her team left a lasting impression and actively affected the paper the next school year as many of them stayed on for newer roles, and writers she trained as EIC chose to join the team. Shannon looked after a group of editors and writers her own age, and her role taught her how to manage her peers.

"Even though I'm peers with these people, I have to kind of rise above that," Shannon reflected. For example, she may have to tell an editor: "In a lot of ways, I am your boss, and I do want to make sure that you're doing the job. And I know that's difficult to hear, but I am really struggling with you in this way."

The complex process showed Shannon how to speak up for how she feels about things—to learn how to be a woman taking up space, vocalize how she feels, and not think small. Student leadership and a school paper can help prepare women to stand up for what they believe in and to speak their opinions to their peers. Starting in high school or college can help develop these skills for the workspace one day. It's a skill that takes time to blossom and grows over time with mentors' help. Mentors can come in all shapes, sizes, and titles. I would consider Shannon a mentor for me at this point in my life, and the editors at *Rolling Stone* were her mentors. It's a cycle of abundance when done correctly.

"It's gonna feel like you're being really harsh and hot-headed and bossy with people, but it's going to be so much more effective," Shannon said. "If you're like: 'Look, I am your boss. I need this to be done. And if it's not done, then this isn't going to work out. I'm sorry like I can't do it for you anymore.' I think that's like something that I really had to learn."

School papers have the potential for individual growth as we start to find our pace in the journalism industry. Practicing makes for a better result later on, so start learning how to be innovative, to be a manager, and to be able to speak up for yourself (and your beliefs) sooner rather than later. Create a strong voice and mature it as one that will not be silenced.

The Importance of Smaller Internships

We have covered how our first job can have potential and what we can learn from school papers, but Shannon offered even more insight into how small internships can start our journalism industry journey.

A smaller internship is when you work for a company that doesn't have a million Instagram followers. *I'm kidding.* Smaller internships land us the more prominent roles that we have our eyes set on. If we dream about working for *The New York Times* one day, then a smaller internship could be at a local newspaper. An NBC News internship can be considered small. It's all about perspective and how we define success, and everyone measures success differently. We can define our internships by what we get out of them. They can give us new skills, connections, or inspiration. The real challenge of "smaller" internships is how we will use them to get us to the next step.

Shannon had a smaller internship with *Bandsintown* that helped her land her more significant internship at her dream workplace, *Rolling Stone Magazine*. She also interned at the *New York Daily News (NYDN)* in between those internships. Shannon covered crime in the city during her time working at the *New York Daily News*.

"It was a great internship in a lot of ways 'cause it taught me to write five articles a day and really fast," Shannon reflected. "It taught [me] AP style really quickly. I think it taught me a lot about how a newsroom works."

Shannon says her internship at the *NYDN* helped guide her to where she belongs, in part by confirming that she does not belong on a crime beat. Her lack of knowledge about crime and the courts hindered her reporting there, she says, but it enabled her to improve her writing skills. Shannon walked away with industry connections and bragging rights to having worked at a major news publication. Now, Shannon is pursuing her path toward a career in the industry that she is passionate about, and her small internships helped to illuminate it.

Origins Have Unique Advantages within Themselves

Our origin can be a crucial factor when thinking about the unique advantages we can bring to the journalism industry table. Whether we are in NYC, California, Boston, or a small town in Wyoming, our point of origin is where we start and where we grow from. The location and culture we grew up around have helped create who we are as a person and will undoubtedly affect us as journalists.

Shannon grew up in Alaska and moved to New York City. She knew she wanted to end up in NYC for journalism, and the city goes hand in hand with the industry. Everything comes together within the hustle and bustle of the city. It's a playground for journalists looking for their next breaking news story or trend to appear. Shannon knew this when she began looking for schools in the city and found a unique opportunity with TKC.

"I really wanted to find a place that was small [and] that I could really thrive in because I wanted to contribute to my student newspaper," Shannon said. "I know at big schools [it] can be hard to do because there are so many people. When you make New York connections, that's going to go really far. Connections that you make in New York are going to really get you far. There are so many programs that you can do where you can do New York study abroad."

Shannon wanted bylines quickly, and she wanted them to count. People are shocked at her experiences when she goes to conferences as a college student. Every city has its own unique opportunities, not just New York City. National newsrooms are always looking for writers from "out of town" to cover their local sections. We have the advantage of knowing the area we grew up in or have lived in, increasing coverage for it. We become valuable.

If *The New York Times* needs to cover an event happening in Texas, it may lean toward giving the job to a reporter from the area. I am from the Dallas area, and if I am looking for work in the city, I can pull in my perspective from being raised in north Texas and understanding the culture. Shannon's Alaskan heritage and the unique culture she grew up around give her a distinctive perspective to work from. She can offer insights into Alaska that someone from the south cannot, and vice-versa.

"Being from Alaska has helped me so much with so many stories," Shannon said.

No one in this world has had a combination of the same upbringing, same origin, and the same experiences. Everyone has a contrasting perspective they can use to their advantage, and how they use it is also unique. It's essential to take a moment to consider what the combination of our background, origin, and current locations can offer us before we quickly dismiss it. Once we understand how important these aspects are to us as writers, we can learn how to make ourselves and our work marketable and profitable.

After graduation, Shannon plans to return to Juneau, Alaska. She is taking on a new communications role in the local area but still plans to freelance for New York City companies. She will get to offer her unique talents to her hometown and share her heritage with others from there. Shannon shows no signs of slowing down anytime soon.

When she arrives in Juneau, her goal is to start a podcast featuring Alaskan Native elders, and she hopes to make a documentary about growing up in Alaska with interviews and stories based on her own family. I know students at King's have learned from Shannon in her time at the school, and if she has taught us anything, it's that we have to start somewhere because we never know where we could end up.

"There is no harm in just going for something even if you don't think you're qualified for it," Shannon offered as advice.

"It's not gonna make you look bad; if anything, it's going to make you look good."

If we ever feel vulnerable about getting involved and putting ourselves out there, we have to remember that we are not the only ones. People like Shannon are within schools. They are willing to help us write, improve our skills, and be there for us as we endure a vast learning experience. It's time to start our journeys and see where they take us.

As Shannon likes to say, "It's a great day to be a journalist." It's also a great day to pack the car up, start it, and take off on the road to your goals and dreams.

CHAPTER FIVE

EXPAND YOUR VISION

Every time I take a cab from the Financial District in Manhattan to LaGuardia Airport in Queens, I pass through the Queens-Midtown tunnel. The eighty-year-old passageway burrows deep beneath the East River to connect Midtown Manhattan and Long Island, Queens. From the backseat of a yellow taxi, the tunnel seems narrow, cramped, and—in gridlocked traffic—endless. It's also very, very dark until you reach the other end. Then, especially on a sunny day, the sunshine will blind you as you emerge from the portal and into the city.

Sometimes people stay in their tunnels without realizing it. They get so focused on the darkness that they fail to see the light at the end, much less imagine what could be on the other side.

Brands, companies, content creators, writers, and well, anyone can get stuck in this tunnel vision. When we do, we fail to see the opportunity waiting on the other side of it—the new "lightness" of what can be. But when we expand our vision beyond the tunnel, we almost always find the light. The tunnel is just the time in between what was before and what lies ahead.

I want to introduce you to two people who had the foresight to look beyond their tunnel vision. One went beyond the fabric laid out before her, and another saw an opportunity to create the life she wanted. Their stories shed some light on *how* and *why* we strive to expand our vision beyond the tunnel's concave walls.

If you follow the annual *Forbes* 30 Under 30 announcements, you may recognize the name Lindsay Peoples Wagner. *Forbes* named the *Teen Vogue* editor-in-chief to its 30 Under 30 in Media list for 2020 in recognition of her work in media and journalism.[15] Seven years after she worked as a *Teen Vogue* fashion assistant, Lindsay took on the role of editor-in-chief of the magazine.

Formerly a fashion editor for New York Media's *The Cut*, she worked on articles, styled shoots, and assisted the fashion department when needed. She started her column and even won the American Society of Magazine Editors Next Award, which honors outstanding achievements by magazine journalists under the age of thirty. Stella Bugbee, the current editor-in-chief and president of *The Cut*, nominated her for the award in 2017.[16]

Dating back to 2010, Lindsay worked as a Levi Strauss & Co. styling and public relations intern, a freelance public relations assistant for the Starworks Group, a *Teen Vogue* fashion assistant intern, and a fashion news writer for *Beauty and the Dirt*. She also freelanced as a fashion assistant and writer for *O, The Oprah Magazine*.[17]

---

15 "Lindsay Peoples Wagner, 29," Forbes Media, accessed June 19, 2020.
16 "Winners of 2017 ASME Next Awards Announced," American Society of Magazine Editors, published February 2, 2017.
17 "Lindsay Peoples Wagner," LinkedIn, accessed June 19, 2020.

Lindsay also worked as a fashion market assistant for *Teen Vogue* and a fashion market reporter for *Style.com*, then found her way to *The Cut* as a fashion market editor. Lindsay returned to *Teen Vogue* as the lady in charge in October 2018. The EIC has had quite the journey to get to where she is today.[18]

Her vision as an editor-in-chief is refreshing. Lindsay looks to "restructure and rebrand [the] magazine to focus on fashion, beauty, politics, and identity." This idea has been implemented in the content, but also the staff she manages. The staff under Linsday is focused on the mission of *Teen Vogue*.[19]

"I'm really looking for someone who is hungry to do the work and less thirsty for attention," Lindsay commented.[20]

Lindsay's EIC role has opened a door for her to influence culture and give a platform to younger people, something other media companies may not do. This is something I have watched firsthand with the publication. The *Teen Vogue* of my teenage years placed a strong focus on materialistic things, but when I received a promotional email in 2020, I noticed a strong difference. The magazine shares political coverage and topics that matter to their audience around the nation. Lindsay wanted to emphasize this as an EIC.[21]

Teenagers today are outspoken and politically active. They use their voices to talk about what matters to them and what they are fighting for. They care about LGBTQIA+ rights, the presidential election, climate change, and more. *Teen Vogue* empowers the visions of this generation by expanding their coverage beyond fashion trends.

---

18   Ibid.
19   *Teen Vogue*, "Teen Vogue's Editor-In-Chief Explains Her Career Path, from First Job to Current | Teen Vogue," August 22, 2019, video, 11:58.
20   *Teen Vogue*, "Teen Vogue's Editor-In-Chief Explains Career Path."
21   Ibid.

Under Lindsay's leadership, the magazine reached a new maturity level. Not every EIC would jump into a balanced system of coverage for fashion, beauty, politics, and identity. *Teen Vogue's* influence expanded beyond the tunnel vision they previously had to reach a bigger audience.

The print side of journalism is stuck in its tunnel. I consistently received one comment when I would tell people I wanted to be a journalist: "Well, print journalism is dying, so good luck." Is print journalism "dying," or are we just having to reinvent parts of its wheel?

Print journalism includes newspapers and magazines. It is a collection of reports and stories shared with the general public through the designated medium. Some journalists may not prefer print for its deadlines and limited operating spaces, but the medium has created some of the most compelling and riveting stories.

Newspapers and magazines cannot afford to make a mistake, and if they do, it is an expensive fix.[22] Print media also creates different jobs for people. We need writers, editors, layout designers, photographers, advertisement coordinators, and more. Publishers and owners across the country have faced the challenge of finding ways to keep their print newspapers and magazines alive and fighting.

Carole Sprunk inspires me. As a founder, owner, publisher, director, writer, and mother, she's a woman who does it all. Her book *Seed Money: From Doubt to Clout* is about adversity, entrepreneurship, and creating a portfolio mindset. She is the owner and publisher of *Edge Magazine* in Nebraska, but she also owns another business. She founded her business,

---

22 "Difference Between Online and Print Journalism," Hosbeg (Blog), accessed May 11, 2020.

Clout Coffee, as a way to empower and encourage others in their lives every day through fresh coffee beans.[23] She also serves as a director of agency development.[24] *Carole is quite the businesswoman.*

She first got involved in the newspaper and printing industry in 2012. Her journey toward being owner and publisher of *Edge* felt natural to her. Magazine publishing is a big passion of hers, and when the founder of *Edge* decided to sell, she couldn't help but want to get involved. A business broker listed the magazine for sale, and Carole's former employer looked at the magazine as a business investment opportunity but did not have much interest in purchasing. On the other hand, Carole loved it and saw a future with it.

"I believe in sharing good news," Carole stated. "When I saw this magazine, I fell in love with it because it was good from cover to cover. It made me feel good. It made my heart happy."

Carole put in a bid to buy the magazine. She relentlessly pursued the business deal even when they told her "no" multiple times. "No" was not the answer she would settle for and would not be the end of her attempts to buy the magazine. She wanted something of her own that she could be proud of at the end of the day, and after a year and a half of negotiations, she officially owned the magazine.

Edge Magazine claims to be "West Omaha's Premier Lifestyle Publication" with a focus on covering the community around it. Carole's passion for printing and love for Omaha are infused in the publication.[25] When she worked for a pub-

---

23 "About Clout," Clout Coffee, accessed September 30, 2020.
24 "Carole Sprunk," LinkedIn, accessed June 21, 2020.
25 "About Us," Edge Magazine, accessed June 21, 2020.

lisher who released two weekly newspapers, Carole's passion project focused on getting newspapers in the hands of community. Carole had a goal of educating the next generation through reading materials, current events, interactive content, and consumable media. As the leader of *Edge*, she put a major focus on sharing the stories of the community's youth.

Have a Good Mindset

We cannot be afraid to start new things when trying to build up to something; begin at the bottom, and build up to the top. We have to be willing to find our purpose and search for the drive to take a passion for something tangible.

"I think everything that I do leverages each other, and at the end of the day, the purpose behind everything is to just be of service and to help others," Carole commented.

The way she sees it: once we find purpose in what we are doing, we can balance anything we set our minds to. If we focus on what matters to others, finding stories to share and inform people will come naturally. It's time to go beyond what we want and to dig into the minds of others. Listen to them when they talk, and let it be a guide for choosing what we want to cover as journalists.

If we are focused on ourselves, then we won't find the right story. Ask yourself and contrast what people want and what they need to hear. Expand your vision to try and see what matters to others, and have a positive attitude going into it.

Build Up the Value of a Team

Carole's official title may be publisher and owner, but she sees herself as a team lead and liaison. Carole's team helps keep everything in balance, and while she does not have a journalism background, she knows how to find people who do. She sees her role as an opportunity to champion a team, develop them, and make them feel empowered to do their job correctly and efficiently.

Carole noted that "recognizing their strengths and weaknesses, and complimenting them," is important as a team leader.

"Your team is valuable to you," Carole said. "So, thank them for what they do and appreciate them and understand that they're humans with families."

The team at *Edge Magazine* is a mixture of original employees and those who Carole has hired since taking control. Carole learned how to integrate different people and become the leader of her team. As said before, she considers what matters to them and expanded her vision past what she needs from her employees. She thinks about how she can empower them.

If we are on a team or leading a team, then it's essential to recognize the importance of feedback. Writing and reporting requires a certain level of vulnerability. No one wants to do something wrong or incorrectly, but corrections must happen. The key is to make sure your team members know you are correcting things because you care. Look out for each other when we are stuck in different tunnels, and together we can reach the light at the end.

Expand Your Vision

Carole searches for diverse revenue sources for *Edge Magazine* through new ideas. Her tunnel is full of statistics and doubts about making money with the printing industry in a technology-driven society. Carole sees an opportunity to change it.

"You have two choices: you can either succumb to that, or you can change that," Carole said. "If you're stuck in your tunnels zone, you have to expand your vision to let new opportunities come in."

The opportunities are endless when you choose to fight a complacent mindset and use a passion to drive you toward producing what you want to share with the world. New ideas and niches to cover can help expand audience engagement. Taking time to look introspectively at our personal lives means we also have to see beyond any tunnel zone that affects it daily. When we feel stuck or unhappy, there is no better time like the present to do something that we are passionate about. At thirty, Carole had a traditional career but wanted something more. She had two choices: succumb to it or change it.

If we are unsure of making a career-altering decision, then we can first consider a side hustle. Taking that step may mean spending hours a week working without any revenue in the beginning, but we have to find our course. Carole is a huge fan of having the faith in ourselves to follow our passions. A commitment to work toward a passion is an invitation for the future to create itself.

Think Business

A new adventure is waiting for Carole. Her next project is creating an organization for magazine publishers, called Publishers Connect, to create bring together publishers all over the country. Magazine publishers are dealing with the same things, whether in Nebraska, California, or North Carolina. Carole wants to offer her print publishing advice when she can.

"I want to cultivate you because you can do the purpose of your magazine when you have an overall mission for your community because you want to create a magazine," Carole said.

Carole does not think print is dead. She cannot wait to speak to thousands of people about this topic. Carole's big passion for printing comes from its tangibility, interactiveness, and consumability. We can physically hold a printed paper in our hands and skim through the words as needed. We interact with the information we intake differently; we can be inspired, saddened, or have any other emotions. There are not many mistakes, and Carole understands the pain of a fact-check gone wrong.

"If I tell your story on Facebook right now and I screw up, I can edit it, and I didn't miss a beat," Carole said. "If I print your story in my magazine and I screw up, that's about a $7,000 mistake. And the same with newspapers. Print journalism is still, depending on your source, way more credible than digital journalism will ever be."

Keeping print alive is necessary to Carole. Anything can happen when reinventing the wheel—expanding beyond the classic print image to see what new possibilities are ahead. Sharing stories on Facebook doesn't ignite the same feeling of physically holding and seeing an article.

Carole did not wait to jump into her role as an entrepreneur. She dove deep into the industry because she had a passion for it, and she encourages us to do the same. "You do not have to have all the answers right now," Carole said. "Surround yourself with people who have that same mindset because naysayers and negative people and people who say you can't do that do not belong in your headspace. You need to chase it as your life depends on it."

When stuck in a tunnel, imagine what is on the other side. Go beyond the darkness of the tunnel and think about the freedom the lightness presents over there. Make sure the passengers in your vehicle to success feel the same. Think positive, consider what matters to others, and go beyond the expected tunnel. Let's build something through our work or personal life that will mean something to us and others.

CHAPTER SIX

VALUES BUILD A BRAND

What's at the core of Apple's unique ability to sell a phone and gain a brand loyalist?

Apple creates products that help us achieve what we set out to accomplish. Brand loyalists love that they have instant access for communication to family, can connect with friends on social apps, answer work emails outside the office, and capture the moments they want to remember. All from their preferred Apple device.

Apple connects with what people value. Humans are always aimed at achieving something. When a brand can connect with someone's mission in life and produce something that improves their life, then they want to share it with everyone. Brand loyalists become culture influencers when they find a product offering value to their life. They build a community around it, and that creates unique microcultures.

Professor Alissa Wilkinson teaches Principles of Cultural Interpretations (PCI) at The King's College and is also a staff critic for Vox.com. She writes about film, TV, and the arts. Specifically, she looks at their intersection with media, religion, and rhetoric. Professor Wilkinson has taught cinema studies, literature, and cultural theory to students at King's for over a decade.[26] I had the chance to take PCI with her as a college sophomore. Every week in PCI we debated a specific topic that has a distinctive pull on our community and tried to break down why we interact with those subjects in the way we do. We read books like Andy Crouch's *Culture Making: Recovering Our Creative Calling* and *Playing God: Redeeming the Gift of Power*. PCI gave me insight into the motivations that influence behaviors and choices people make every day.

We have a unique connection to value systems and cultures. Our actions move us closer to what desire, and while it differentiates from person to person, we seek to achieve what make us feel accomplished. My go-to question when discussing issues in our lives is "why do you feel that way?" Think beyond the surface level of that answer. Why do we need to feel accomplished? Is it because we value feeling satisfaction or because we have to prove something to ourselves?

What we value, what our culture has taught us to love, and the belief system we build navigate us toward people who share our values and beliefs. Underlying agreeable assumptions connect us to the people closest in our lives. We keep them in our lives because they empower us to follow those desires. This is also for the brands we favor.

Opportunity arises to create loyal consumers with shared value systems. Value and belief systems shape the content we promote, and consumers will share what they feel connected to. Turning consumers into marketers is key to growing engagement in the digital world. One share can turn into multiple more views, and so on.

---

26 "About," Alissa Wilkinson, accessed June 20, 2020.

Iridescent Women is a digital media site on a mission. "We believe every woman is brilliant—uniquely formed and divinely woven together, with the ability to light up this world through goodness and kindness, bravery and resilience," begins the global brand's mission statement. "Her shimmer is multi-faceted and potential uncontainable. Created with purpose, she is destined to shine."[27]

Since its 2018 launch, the brand has grown to include The Iridescent Podcast, Iridescent Perks (*which offers discounts to female-led brands*), webinars, events, and an online shop with merch.[28]

Before cofounding *Iridescent Women* with Alexandra Brown, CEO Nicole Smithee worked in the ministry and nonprofit realm. At nineteen, she joined the staff at a church in Los Angeles, working her way up to senior and executive leadership positions. Nicole then moved to New York City to start a new chapter and work with a nonprofit called the Liberty Foundation.

Nicole put her public speaking skills from her ministry years to get into a larger public speaking realm. Around three summers ago, the idea for *Iridescent Women* came to her while speaking at a young adult's conference. Her lightbulb moment came right before she delivered her message as a keynote speaker. Before stepping onto the stage, Nicole took a moment to embrace the uplifting, encouraging atmosphere.

"It was one of those moments [where] I was just really grateful to be doing what I was doing and really grateful to be there," Nicole reflected. "I was kind of taking that moment

---

27   "About Us," Iridescent Women (Blog), accessed October 11, 2020.
28   Ibid.

of gratitude and praying, and during that moment of prayer, I really felt led."

She felt called to look at the individual faces rather than the big crowd. Nicole noticed all of the young women in the crowd, something clicked, and she felt a desire to do more in the next season of her life. Her mind drifted to herself as she began to think through this new inspiration. What would she have benefitted from in her late teens or twenties, or even her early thirties? What does it look like to be an empowered woman in the twenty-first century?

These questions navigated her brainstorming. Nicole's brainstorming session focused on meeting women where they were rather than having to physically gather at live events. An idea started forming around the ability to share collective experiences globally and leverage technology to do it. The foundation she imagined was a platform by women, for women.

Her ministry, leadership, and executive management background helped navigate Nicole in launching *Iridescent Women* with Alexandra Brown. Nicole did not have a journalism background specifically but felt her knowledge with different assets could help start a digital media company. The team finds individual strengths in other people to help find balance. Launching *Iridescent Women* created an unexpected career pivot for Nicole.

"If you would have told me three or four years ago that I would own a digital media company," Nicole commented, "I would have kind of laughed and said you got the wrong person."

Iridescent Women's values laid the foundation for their branding. They created the site to communicate with women worldwide. Nicole values connecting with an audience through authentic content and is always willing to be humble and learn something new. That is how she built a digital media site without a background in journalism and publishing.

Create Content For Your Audience

Nicole wanted to create opportunities for new and emerging writers. The ideal contributor had to be vulnerable enough to share stories that help bring women together. The *Iridescent Women* team values connecting its audience to different voices from around the world through various media, including written words, videos, and podcasts. Nicole imagined a platform for women to express their insights, discuss their passions, and share their pivotal life moments.

"We really wanted to create something that was a source of encouragement for women and a source of inspiration and ultimately a source of equipping and empowering," Nicole stated.

Iridescent Women content will cover representation in the entertainment industry one day to discussing starting a business from home during quarantine the next. The topics range from culture, spirituality, life, and more. They aim for the content to be hope-filled and authentic. What good would it be if they skipped over the urgent and relevant facts of a woman's life? The ladies of *Iridescent Women* have tried to be innovative to connect with their audience and connect with them in any way they can.

Iridescent Women's audience is composed of their writers and the communities around them with shared values and beliefs. The women involved with the digital media site relate to the brand's mission and share their stories in return. They can connect with women who feel what they feel. They can share it with their friends. It is one big circle of values and beliefs.

Be Humble and Open to Learning

Nicole understands the need to keep her eye out on new trends to stay connected and grow their audience. If it wants to remain relevant, it has to humble itself to see a need for improvement. Every step of *Iridescent Women*'s development since launching has been necessary. It has been able to understand its audience better and see the needs that require attention.

Nicole believes the trends that emerged during the 2020 global pandemic are going to last beyond the period of time. People will want some kind of personal touch and interaction with people who lead the companies they are using, watching, or following. They want to see their community. *Iridescent Women* has to navigate how to connect readers to the truth behind the stories and engage with it. Nicole said they are seeking genuine connections beyond the content they are producing. If anything, it is more personal than ever before.

"I think where digital media companies need to go to stay relevant in the next few years is to find ways in real-time to connect with women," Nicole commented. "We're seeing a lot of innovation, ironically, during the pandemic. These really high-level produced productions are no longer accessible to people, but Jimmy Fallon's still doing a late-night show in his house with his kids, and his wife was a camera person, and we're all watching, and we're loving it. So, I think people are having to get really innovative right now."

Another part of *Iridescent Women* where Nicole looks with humbleness and an eagerness to learn is within the intern team. My first internship was with the brand, and being an intern for *Iridescent Women* is different from other companies. Interns are at the table where things are happening, can offer insights, and can suggest new ideas.

Nicole looks for interns that have a shared value system. She will ask herself about applicants: will they be a good team player? Do they believe in the mission of *Iridescent*? Does it feel like something that resonates within them? Nicole isn't looking for someone who wants an easy internship, but someone willing to dive deep into the mission to produce the best site possible.

"You could be the most skilled person in the world, but if your heart's not in it, then it's kind of not worth it," Nicole said. "I'm really, really proud to say that our team consists of people whose hearts are in it. You can tell the difference, not just in the work that they do, but in the way that we interact together as a team."

The *Iridescent Women* team are in school, work other jobs, and operate remotely most of the time. They are made strong by their belief in the mission of the company. Nicole's gold combo for a team member is an eagerness to learn and the ability to follow through.

"If somebody is not eager to learn [and] they're not humble, then they're not as hungry," Nicole said.

Excitement does not cover up missing deadlines and complicated communication styles. Nicole looks at potential team members for their drive and ability to take initiatives. In a market with hundreds of internships available, you have to

be willing to be the intern that brings something to the table, *not just the coffee. (I wish to clarify that my employers never been asked me to get them a coffee as an intern, and if you have, I am sorry for that experience.)*
"I want your ideas, and I want you to make things better," Nicole said. "I don't want you just to maintain things."

Iridescent Women team members have to be humble, eager to learn and listen to feedback. Feedback helps us understand our audience and evaluate our skills. Negative feedback can cause emotional bruising but is necessary to produce the best content. The first draft is never the final draft. Being appreciative is important when someone just wants to make our work stronger.

"I can absolutely relate as a writer and as a public speaker," Nicole said. "You're putting yourself out there in a unique way. So it's really important to have tough skin and a tender, tender heart. Keep going after the things you want, and then just be humble enough to learn from those moments."

Instead of feeling like someone is taking away our voice, we have to step back and take a moment to see how we can better our skills. We can seize the opportunities that feedback offers to be proactive and to develop continually.

"You gotta be humble, but go for it," Nicole finished. "Don't wait until you think you've got enough skills to do something or you'll never do it."

Create Honest and Authentic Content

When Nicole first hopped on the social media trend, her profiles became an expression of her authentic everyday life. She loved to share the messages she felt were relevant to her followers. As she built a following while preaching and public speaking, she started to value people connecting with her real life, not one she had curated for social media. Nicole finds it natural to share her wins and losses with her audience to complete a picture rather than just showing scenes of her life as an entrepreneur and founder.

"If you only express the wins and not the journey to get there, you make it feel impossible for people to try to pursue the thing in their heart," Nicole said. "I really want people to feel like [you can] go for your dreams, go for the God dreams in your heart. That's really important to me. So being honest about that journey has also been important."

The ability to be vulnerable through content is a good skill to have, and the process can be gratifying when you connect with others that your story has resonated with. *Iridescent Women* built itself off of sharing a unique level of honest and authentic content. As a contributor, I discussed issues like my struggles with my body and image that I held within for years. I published articles that I would have never written without the supportive platform.

It is important to note that these are personal stories and not news articles. While *Iridescent Women* falls into the digital media company, Nicole is the first to say that they would not identify as a journalistic company.

"I think what we do is we highlight the work of journalists and get that in front of women's faces," Nicole stated. "There's so much information that is happening in the world. So we try to curate the news events, specifically when it comes to journalism, the things that journalists are writing about that are very relevant to a woman's life. Then we make sure that those are on our platform."

Nicole noted that making the distinction is essential. She finds it dishonoring to the people who put in the long hours of researching, reporting and fact-checking in their careers to claim to be doing journalism without experience or expertise. That's why *Iridescent Women* focuses on highlighting the work of journalists. The digital media site is looking for a way to leverage their community's voices and invite women to share their experiences. They are not looking to create hard-hitting journalistic stories, but to build a community through blog-style writing.

The balance between news curation and blogging is the team of editors behind the scene. Nicole noted them as the "unsung behind-the-scenes heroes." With so many different voices on different platforms, a level of excellence and professionalism has to be maintained. People can tell the difference between genuine and fake. Nicole never wants an audience member to regard their content that way.

"I think it's good to just provide stuff that feels real, feels relevant, feels helpful for people," Nicole reflected. "Just be true to who you really are and not what you think will get you more followers. We can almost like smell out the difference now cause we've all been doing this long enough."

The ability to put yourself out there is not easy, but a community built upon it is rewarding.

Know Your Values

Iridescent Women encourages women to leave their mark. Their reach is global, with over two hundred unique contributors on the site. They have stayed true to the value system they created as a foundation for the company as a young company.

During the pre-launch stage of creating *Iridescent Women*, Nicole and Alex dedicated a good portion of time and effort to go through the long process of creating their identity.

"I look back on it now and I'm very grateful that we took the time that we did," Nicole reflected. She counts their time spent laying down the foundation of values and branding as a vital decision.

Nicole and Alex spent time articulating how they wanted to narrow down and truly own their site values. They focused on understanding what kind of digital media company they wanted to be, the conversations people were looking for, and what type of experience they would like a woman to have when interacting with them across platforms. They are committed to diverse and real conversations that are practical.[29]

Nicole believes it is shortsighted to think about what will look pretty on Instagram when building a brand. While feed aesthetics play a significant role in attracting followers, developing a concept that will stand out and last the test of time is just as important. Nicole and Alex created the brand with solid foundations that will not change even as it evolves into different iterations. We can paint a house's colors, but we won't tear down and rebuild the structure. What is trending today may not be trending in five years or even five months.

"It's funny how quickly trends change in digital," Nicole said. "I think when you see us, we stand out from other brands, but we still feel relevant for women. Our branding, even before you read an article from us or go to our website, feels vibrant, feels helpful, feels exciting, feels like an ode to the old and the new, and doesn't feel like one age group or doesn't feel like, you know, one kind of woman."

---

29 "Iridescent Values," Iridescent Women (Blog), accessed May 10, 2020.

The big question on digital media entrepreneurs' minds is this: **will I still be relevant next year?** Trends may change, but values do not. Consumers invest in companies and people that share similar values to them. For Nicole, this was a big point for the launch of *Iridescent*. They refuse to promote something only to get eyeballs on it and increase engagement. It has to connect with the company's identity and how it can impact the lives of women. This will never fade.

Nicole Smithee has been a great leader to learn from. She empowers women through her career and continues to do that by leading the *Iridescent Women* team. She created a path because she saw a market opening that she wanted to talk to, and she made it happen.

"I think a lot of times people wait for opportunities to come to their door before they do anything with them and that's too late," Nicole stated. "I think you've got to be proactive and say, 'Hey, let me intern for you or let me write for you.' Ultimately, if you want to be successful in things that you feel really called to, you just gotta put yourself out there before you feel like you know what you're doing and then just commit to learning that as you go," Nicole finished. "You'll get a lot further that way."

When creating a brand, whether company or personal, we have to remember that people connect with the things they value. It's not our job to understand what each person is looking for but to seek a value system that will attract the right people to us.

CHAPTER SEVEN

BET ON YOURSELF

In one of Hollywood's most iconic opening scenes, Audrey Hepburn—as Truman Capote's Holly Golightly—peers into a glitzy Tiffany & Co. window display. There, we later learn, at the bustling corner of Manhattan's Fifth Avenue and 57th Street, The *Breakfast at Tiffany's* character has found her happy place. The beautifully decorated jewelry store, she says, is a quiet and proud-looking place where nothing bad can happen.

"If I could find a real-life place that'd make me feel like Tiffany's, then—then I'd buy some furniture and give the cat a name!"[30]

If Tiffany's is Miss Golightly's *home*, then the newsroom just might be Kimeko McCoy's *Tiffany's*.

"As hectic and as crazy as it was, that's how I felt walking into a newsroom. And I knew that was where I needed to be."

As a high school senior, Kimeko had to shadow someone working in the field or job they wanted to do one day. She chose to follow around Atlanta journalist and news anchor

---

30 "Breakfast at Tiffany's Quotes," Rotten Tomatoes, accessed October 25, 2020.

Ted Hall and recalled the experience being similar to the scene in *Breakfast at Tiffany's*. As crazy and hectic as the newsroom can be, she feels at ease in one.

Kimeko started—or strutted—into the unknown to have her Holly Golightly moment last longer. The unknown path can ignite fear for young women entering the journalism industry. A big question when job searching can be: how do we stand out? Once our resumes and education get us an interview, then how do we land the job? Believing in ourselves is the first step.

Kimeko's interest in journalism started in high school. Growing up, she loved reading books and writing. Her underlying passion is listening to people and learning their stories, and she decided to use her writing skills as a journalist.

Kimeko studied journalism at Georgia Southern University from 2010 to 2014. Her studies focused majorly on print journalism as they had yet to start incorporating digital media into the program. Kimeko researched and did a lot of legwork for stories in her early days interning at local newspapers like *The Marietta Daily Journal* and *The Savannah Morning News*. Post-graduation, she worked for *The George-Anne* newspaper and *The Saint Augustine Record* and also returned to *The Marietta Daily Journal* briefly.[31]

Kimeko took the time during these transitions to dip her foot into new waters: social media. During her short time as a reporter for the *Cherokee Ledger-News* in Canton, Georgia, she had the chance to work as a social media editor. Kimeko discovered a new passion for the journalism world's digital side.

Working on the digital side opened a new door for Kimeko as an audience development specialist position at

---

[31] "Kimeko McCoy," LinkedIn, accessed June 21, 2020.

the *Atlanta Journal-Constitution*. She developed as a multimedia journalist and moved to New York City to join Adweek as a social media editor. In 2019, she started at the Turner Broadcasting System, Inc., as a digital marketing specialist.[32]

Kimeko's unique path post-college guided her to become a well-rounded multimedia journalist and, five years later, is still writing while dipping into digital media. Her belief in her abilities kept her in the game. She loved her first job as a feature writer and felt lucky getting to produce stories that matter to people. Her transition from feature writer to beat reporting changed her mind about digital media.

"I make the joke that I moved into digital media kicking and screaming," Kimeko joked. "'Cause once I kind of understood it, I understood the importance of it and kind of pushed the newsroom into doing that."

I found Kimeko through a website called Journalism Internships and their mentorship program. The Media Mentors program is available for students interested in audio and radio, data/investigative journalism, audience engagement, general reporters and editors, sports, broadcast, news design, photo/video, public relations, marketing, product, and engineering. *So, pretty much everything in the industry.*[33]

Kimeko offers help in the audience engagement category, and it said she could "coach on project management, social media innovation, being WOC in media and feature writing."[34] I quite literally found and approached her through social media because she seemed like someone I could

---

32 Ibid.
33 "Introducing Media Mentors," Adriana Lacy, Journalism Mentors, published October 16, 2019, accessed June 21, 2020.
34 "Media Mentors: Audience Engagement," Journalism Mentors, accessed June 21, 2020.

connect with. Kimeko is someone you feel comfortable with immediately. Her warm personality and humor can shine through a phone call. She has paved her path into the industry as a digital marketer, media coordinator, and freelance writer. Her journey exemplifies how ever-changing and evolving different roles are in the industry. One day we are reporters, and the next, we could be doing social media and online audience engagement. *Sometimes even on the same day.* Ultimately, we have to go with the flow of the industry and see where the tide takes us.

Don't Compare

Kimeko first started at local papers in Georgia, and she often found herself to be the only woman, or more specifically, the only Black woman in the newsroom. She felt privileged to be able to go to school, work at internships for free, and start networking at a younger age than some. Kimeko learned how to pull her weight quickly in a newsroom. Still, Kimeko couldn't help but compare herself to others.

During her first job after graduating college, Kimeko attended an Online News Association (ONA) conference. The digital media organization focuses on audience development and digital reporters with a small focus on print journalism. The first year Kimeko found out about the big conference, she felt heartbroken.

"There were people who were the same age as me working at *The New York Times*, working at the *Los Angeles Times*, *Chicago Tribune*, and things like that," Kimeko reflected. "And I was just like, oh my God, I'm not doing enough."

Her dad quickly to jumped in as she dealt with these emotions and comparisons. He reminded Kimeko to embrace her current chapter and experience as a feature writer and getting her leg up as a reporter. She had time to write about the important things and energize her passions. People working in digital media were pushing out content like crazy, and as Kimeko put it, "kind of working at these content mills" to get multiple articles a day published. Others were fighting to get their foot into a door along with every other college student who graduated recently.

Kimeko's dad encouraged her to be a big fish in a little pond without comparing herself to others. She needed to see the importance of her work and embrace the opportunity she had in that moment.

"You're working at a smaller paper and there's less resources and there's less people," Kimeko said in reflecting on her conversation with her dad. "The work that you're doing has made you recognized in your little community."

Kimeko had invitations to speak at college events and participate in panels for local journalists. Her name started to be recognized she published her work. It can be very easy in the journalism industry to start comparing everything about ourselves to others.

We have to rid ourselves of negative thoughts. Everyone's job means has meaning and purpose. Whether we are in the big city or our local small towns, when we start comparing ourselves to others, then we might lose sight of the goal in front of us and why we are journalists in the first place: to tell the stories of those around us.

Every day I read a mantra out loud to myself while looking in the mirror. I end it with "I am not led astray by my own doubts or others." We cannot let any doubts we create in our heads control our actions. A whole world is out there for us when we break free from any negative thoughts and comparisons, and I invite you to join me on the journey.

Don't Make Yourself Small

A job is what we make it, and we are given ample opportunities to continually better our own crafts. Kimeko quickly learned what type of writing she preferred when she went from a feature reporter to a city beat reporter. This style of reporting didn't excite her, and she had to push out multiple stories a day. In an attempt to balance her reporting, Kimeko got involved with social media and digital marketing as a reporter.

"I kind of pitched myself and I said, what can we do here?" Kimeko commented. "I'd love to partner. I'd love to work. And they said, you know, actually our sister paper is hiring. If you want to move over there and work on the digital efforts and have kind of a more digital role with reporting being in the background. I said yeah, absolutely. So I did that and then I kind of fell in love with it."

Kimeko began working more behind the scenes. She helped get reporters on social media, created their mini-brand with them, and worked with digital editing and homepage management. Eventually, social media became the forefront of Kimeko's work, and she loved it. She would never have figured out her passion for audience development if she hadn't taken a chance on herself to try and learn something new.

"Do not make yourself small," Kimeko stated. "I know being young and starting in the industry, especially being a woman, you're often taught or your understanding is, *I just need to put my head down and get this work done and then I'll be promoted.* I think it's important to advocate for yourself and don't be afraid to speak up. If you're good at something, say that you're good at it. If there's a wall in front of you… go around, go over, go under, just push forward as best as you can. No one is going to advocate for you like you."

The journalism industry isn't easy. It never has been and probably never will be. We have to make ourselves big and believe we are worth every unique chance to prove it. Bet on yourself when no one else does. The supporters will join when they feel the confidence radiating off of us and our work. People who choose to count on us to provide are there because they believe in us.

It won't always be easy. Kimeko noted that a "cry stall" will be waiting for us on the hard days. There can be a lot of pressure and emotions, which is okay. We let it out, stand back up, and get ready to start again.

"There's one stall that is designated," Kimeko said. "So if you're just going through it… and you're just crying, let it out."

A cry stall is the specific area of a bathroom designated for those breakdowns, and I find it to be quite fascinating. *It's a unique way of women supporting women.* There are people in the industry like Kimeko, and the other mentors, hoping to lessen cry stall sessions. First step: stop making ourselves seem small.

Don't Hide Your Personality

I grew up with social media documenting every aspect of my life, from favorite songs to Friday Night Lights. My digital carbon footprint is quite large at this point, and somehow, I always struggle with showing my personality online. I want to engage with people without my fear of oversharing getting in the way. Growing up, teachers and mentors told me to keep my social media as bland and professional as possible as to not to deter me from future opportunities.

"I feel like that's a super old-school mentality," Kimeko said. "You can just use [tweets and comments] as a networking tool, you know? 'Cause it shows like you have a brand, but also you have a personality. Nobody wants to follow a robot all day."

A difference exists between your branding and your personality. If someone wants the news about what's going on in Washington, then they will follow the *Washington Post*. If they want something with more color, then they will follow a local Washington reporter to get the latest on what's going on personally.

Being confident in our work and betting on ourselves includes allowing some personality to shine through on social media. We have to let people connect with us. Stop worrying about what others think and find a balance to infuses your brand with personality. We can achieve this by combining different aspects of marketing, audience development, and journalism.

"As long as you have [some] kind of a brand that falls within some categories [and] I think as long as you find that balance, you're good," Kimeko commented. "Don't be afraid to show a little bit your personality."

We have to make it clear to our audience what they can come to our profile to find. Pick a lane and drive full force down it. If we are sports journalists, then we make it clear to our audience that our content is a home base for them to find information on a subject. We can also talk about the things we invest our time and passion in, the newest TV show released, our opinion on a food combination, or a fall trend that should not make a comeback. Showing hints of our personality does not take away from the content we are posting.

"I think right now... in this moment specifically, journalism is going through a huge reckoning," Kimeko said. "I think there are a lot of people who have made rumblings before about the pay disparities between gender, between race, between job descriptions, you know, about the difference between being a reporter and a digital content creator and things like that. You need to be able to work with your reporters. You need to listen to your minority reporters, need to bring more of them into the newsroom and promote them into places where they can make the decisions. So you don't have crazy headlines or pictures that are not true to the story and things like that."

Kimeko predicts some massive tweaks coming to the industry, and newer journalists need to prepare for it. Now more than ever, we have to be confident in who we are and choose to bet on ourselves with whatever changes are coming our way. The industry shows no signs of slowing down its evolution. Make yourself a big fish and show your personality. Be approachable online and build a community around you. We live in a time when people follow *you* and will read your work wherever you post it. *Instantly, or delayed.*

We have to bet that on the fact that we are *the* people for the job. Great risk brings great reward. We can be on ourselves to be the one to take on new pitches, positions, and questions. For example, audiences can look to us for answers on social media if we are approachable. People will naturally seek us out for our expertise when we are confident to answer them.

Approachable digital profiles are full of personality. People want personality and vulnerability on social media. It's time to develop a community mindset with our social media and engage in conversations with the community.

Kimeko McCoy has this down to a science and worked her way up to her position today from her starting point. The beginning of her career didn't involve digital media, but when it came time to make the switch, she bet on herself to be the one leading the way for those around her.

It's time to bet on yourself. Go for the position you want, pitch the cool article, or ask to learn more about a new specification. The world is ours to take, and that is something I am willing to bet on.

PART THREE

THE ADVICE

CHAPTER EIGHT

BE COURAGEOUS

The Syrian government actively blocked foreign journalists from attempting to report on the Syrian civil war in 2012. This didn't stop Marie Colvin from crossing the border. If you're familiar with her name, you'll recognize Marie's conflict zone reporting and the eye patch that masked her battle scar.[35]

In a CNN interview from the city of Homs, near Syria's western border with Lebanon, the veteran war correspondent described "merciless shelling and sniper attacks against civilians."[36] Still, she continued her coverage. Marie believed her presence as one of the few western journalists in the war zone provided a vital line of communication to the rest of the world. It was, she said, one of the worst conflicts she had ever seen. And she had seen dozens of conflicts in her twenty-six-year career as a war correspondent.

Reporting for *The Sunday Times* in London, Colvin covered wars wherever they were. She met with heads of states and military leaders, but her reports focused on the impact

---

35 Marie's Story," Marie Colvin Memorial Foundation, accessed October 1, 2020.
36 Ibid.

wars had on a civilian population. Colvin regarded this as her "moral responsibility" and said it would be "cowardly to ignore them."[37]

Oftentimes, those stories had been hidden, and powerful interests pressured Colvin to ignore them. Whatever the threat, she refused to back down from her reporting. In 2001, while working in Sri Lanka, a grenade shrapnel blinded her in one eye.[38] Her black eye patch post-injury became her trademark badge of honor.

When recalling the event in an address in 2010, Colvin said: "I had gone to the northern Tamil area from which journalists were banned and found an unreported humanitarian disaster. As I was smuggled back across the internal border, a soldier launched a grenade at me and the shrapnel sliced into my face and chest. He knew what he was doing."[39]

Colvin didn't slow down from doing her work, and fighting to tell the truth cost her everything. In February 2012, Colvin died when Syrian forces bombed the makeshift media center she reported from. Colvin actively covered the suffering of civilians in Homs, and she wanted to share the silenced voices despite the dangers she knew were waiting for her upon arrival.[40] Her life ended during a time when she put courage first.

In her final message to her editor before her death, she said, "Will keep trying to get out the information."[41] Even in

---

37 Ibid.
38 *ABC News*, "Telling legendary journalist Marie Colvin's story in 'A Private War,'" November 8, 2018, video, 8:29.
39 "Truth at All Costs," Marie Colvin Memorial Foundation, accessed October 1, 2020.
40 "Marie's Story," Marie Colvin Memorial Foundation, accessed October 1, 2020.
41 Ibid.

the moments before her death, Marie refused to back down from what she saw as her duty.

Colvin's biographer, Lindsey Hilsum, wrote a *Financial Times* article in February 2019 about how she felt "confronted with the reality of Marie, one week tramping through snow and mud in the mountains of Chechnya in fear for her life, and the next chatting to Warren Beatty at an LA party."[42] Colvin lived life to the fullest when she had the chance.

A Private War, a film based on the journalist's career, is not a detailed Colvin biography. The producers tried to capture the war correspondent's fearless image and connect people to Colvin's passion for the truth. I attended a showing of the feature film, and left feeling inspired as a journalist. Her story can, and will, continue to inspire young journalists.

An ABC News segment from November 2018 described Colvin's personal mission as: "to bear witness to the horrors of war" and "giving a voice to the voiceless despite the undeniable risk."[43] *A Private War* is viewed as a homage to Colvin's work and the work of journalists around the world fighting for the truth every day in safe and dangerous conditions. The movie's director, Matt Heineman, said the film is to honor those who are "shedding light on the dark corners of the world."[44]

The Twenty Second Principle

In the movie *We Bought a Zoo*, they discuss the twenty second principle. It's the theory that "sometimes all you need

---

42   Lindsey Hilsum, "Marie Colvin—the making of a myth," *Financial Times*, February 5, 2019.
43   *ABC News*, "Telling legendary journalist Marie Colvin's story."
44   Ibid.

is twenty seconds of insane courage. Just literally twenty seconds of just embarrassing bravery. And I promise you, something great will come of it."[45]

Catherine Plano believes this is the difference between living and existing. She states that if something scares us so much that we restrain ourselves from attempting it, then maybe it is the exact thing we need to go after.[46]

"Bravery is vulnerability. And vulnerability is truth."[47]

It's okay to be scared because it means we care deeply about something. Caring profoundly is where we find our passions, and it dictates the moments we decide to make the changes needed in our lives. What truly matters is how we allow these feelings to guide our decisions.

Twenty seconds can seem like a small piece of time within our day. Every day we have 86,400 seconds to make our day count; to fill it with tasks, memories, and the moments that make us happy.

It takes twenty seconds to decide to make that phone call, send that application, or tackle whatever is standing in between us and our success. We have the power to choose to be courageous and be free from the restrictions of fear. If we let fear control our lives, are we living or just existing? If we let courage guide us, then our potential is limitless.

Serena Tuomi wears a bracelet all the time that quotes this inspirational idea of twenty seconds of insane courage. She has had it through her transition from her hometown in

---

45 Benjamin Mee," Goodreads, accessed June 20, 2020.
46 Catherine Plano, "Twenty Seconds of Insane Courage…," *Medium* (blog), November 10, 2019.
47 Ibid.

Minnesota to New York City—a journey that has held many courageous moments for her.

    As a young kid, Serena loved to read and write. She can even recall when her sixth-grade teacher had her students write a letter to themselves about their dreams. This teacher promised to mail the letters back to them when they were seniors in high school. Serena opened hers right before she moved to NYC. She had written down that she wanted to be an author living in the city. *Well, sixth-grade Serena may have been on to something.*

    Serena found inspiration through her older sister, who is also a journalist and author. Learning from her sister, Serena started her blog in high school to develop her writing skills. Her blog centered around her lifestyle, which included her diagnosed eating disorder; her blog discussed food wellness and recovery. Serena saw the blog as a saving grace.

    As her high school years came to a close, Serena looked at two different paths: going to The King's College (TKC) for journalism or to New York University for nutrition studies. She had a big passion for both subjects and debated back and forth on which one she should make her primary focus.

    As she sorted through which one would be the best path for her, Serena visited NYC by herself a day after turning eighteen. *What a way to ring in being an official adult.* The small-town Minnesota girl saw the Big Apple all by herself without her parents. The trip required a certain level of responsibility, but Serena felt confident she could handle it. Serena felt determined to figure out where her passions would guide her in a city she loved.

    "Traveling alone absolutely gave me this incredible confidence in myself that I'd never had before," Serena noted. "I fell in love with New York at that point. It was just a transformative trip for me."

Serena decided to test out her journalism skills the summer after graduating high school. She got her professional start with an internship at her local newspaper, *Hometown Focus*, and spent her summer reporting on the local events and news. Serena got a taste for what life as a reporter looked like.

Her summer internship played a role in Serena deciding to study journalism at The King's College, living out her sixth-grade self's dream.

She moved to NYC and started school in the fall of 2018. Serena jumped right into being involved at King's and joined the school newspaper, the *Empire State Tribune*. Serena enjoyed writing but had a weird relationship with journalism; she loved writing, but not reporting.

"I'm not into mainstream journalism," Serena said. "What I see as mainstream is mostly like politics, sports, business, and economics."

Her disinterest in these subjects and topics lead to her feeling lost in the journalism major, and she ultimately changed her major to English to focus on writing. This switch didn't last too long because Serena changed back by the end of the semester. Her love for writing didn't outweigh her disinterest in poetry and Shakespeare.

I find it essential to note Serena's switching majors because it shows that the path to journalism degrees aren't always the same. It didn't click right away. She had to keep searching for her place in the industry and finding what she liked to write about. So, that's what she did. Serena set out to find what she wanted to write about and how to be successful at it. She slowly fell back in love with journalism, and the opportunities came her way.

Be Open to New Opportunities

Serena's time at *Hometown Focus* guided her as a young, high school journalist. She reported on what her editor assigned, and her first assignment focused on the one hundredth anniversary of her high school.

"I just remember how overwhelming it was," Serena stated. "That article took me forever and I was like, 'I'm already over this and this is my first article.' I remember sitting in a coffee shop for hours one day to write this really short article; just rewriting it over and over again, and feeling like I just didn't even know my own voice at all."

Her *Hometown Focus* time helped her figure out what journalism truly encompassed and how to find her voice. She did the grunt work to lay the foundations for her stories to come.

Serena started a food nutrition and wellness blog in high school but struggled at the beginning of college to find her footing in journalism. A light came at the end of the tunnel where her two passions combined. The *Empire State Tribune* editor-in-chief, Shannon Mason, saw this passion and approached Serena with the offer to start her own column for the paper during her sophomore year.

Serena's column ended up being about food, and she covered things like Australian cafe culture and cookies for Valentine's Day. Serena had the freedom to choose what she wanted to write about—something different from her initial journalism job.

"She didn't ask me to write anything specific," Serena said. "It was all up to me, which was exciting and like scary at the same time."

If Serena had given up on journalism in the beginning, then she would never have ended up writing her own column about a topic she is passionate about. If we stay closed off to opportunities, then we won't figure out what we ultimately thrive at doing.

Put Yourself Out There

Serena works as an intern for digital media company *Iridescent Women*. She met Nicole Smithee, the CEO of *Iridescent Women*, at a King's College job and internship fair. Serena happened to be working the event, and during set up, she struck up a conversation with Nicole.

"She was just a sweetheart," Serena recalled. "I just remember thinking, 'you are such a ray of sunshine.' She has such a deep heart for women and for inspiring and loving them. I remember telling her I was interested, [and that] I'd love to get an internship at some point, but I couldn't handle it that semester."

Nicole understood Serena's conflicts and told her to reach back out in the spring if things were not as overwhelming. At the beginning of 2020, Serena found Nicole's contact information in her belongings and decided to take a chance on reaching out because she knew how much she wanted to work with Nicole. After reaching out, Serena and Nicole had set up a time and date to meet.

"I just remember telling her all the things I wanted to learn and how I already had a piece in mind because I done an interview with somebody that I'd been waiting to write a story on. I just didn't know where to pitch it," Serena commented. "She was like super excited because the woman that I interviewed with [was] someone that she was like, I've been wanting to get an interview with her in *Iridescent* for so long… It worked out perfectly. And that's how I got started at *Iridescent*."

Serena put herself out there not only for an internship, but also for her first article with the digital media site. The article, "The Hungry Blonde Talks Blogging, Food Freedom, and Faith," is about Gracie Gordon, also known as Hungry Blonde. Gracie is a New York-based food and lifestyle blogger. Gordon had been Serena's favorite blogger since she started her own, and she looked to her for inspiration.

Serena reached out through Instagram's direct messages and pitched Gracie the article idea. The long shot turned into an opportunity when Gracie responded with a yes. The Hungry Blonde and Serena met up at Hu Kitchen in Union Square for the interview. The meeting left Serena on cloud nine.

Serena landed her internship and an interview with her personal inspiration through the twenty seconds of courage it took to press the send button on her messages.

Make the Most Out of Internships

As an *Iridescent Women* team member, Serena has been writing blog-style posts and personal reflection pieces as a writing intern. She is also in charge of scheduling posts on WordPress and publishing items on the website with graphics and details. She will send out social media kits, which are the article graphics for different platforms, to writers when their post is scheduled to publish with instructions on sharing posts and links to the articles. Serena even developed an

FAQ page for the site and worked on new projects for the digital site. Essentially, she's a jack-of-all-trades for the team. Serena has a lot of responsibility on the communications side when dealing with new contributors, current writers, and the overall community by collecting stories, helping people brainstorm, and sending out a monthly newsletter with article ideas. Serena has a goal to dip her feet into the graphic design and editing side, but for now, she is growing in the area she is at.

Serena took her opportunity with *Iridescent Women* to develop new skills. As an intern, she has had the chance to learn different aspects of a digital media site. Interns have a unique opportunity to jump into the industry with a fresh pair of eyes. We are very impressionable initially, and it will help shape us as journalists, so take this unique time to push yourself to explore new things. We never know what we will learn and the door it will lead to.

Set Goals and Aspirations

The 2020-21 school year is Serena's senior year of college. She has her eye set on a few different things and paths for her post-grad career. One of the paths includes the Fulbright Scholar Program. The program offers research, study, and teaching opportunities for recent graduates and graduate students in the United States. The program has 140 countries that you can travel to.[48] The application process has many layers, but if the end result leads you to Europe, I don't know how much we can complain.

---

48 About," Fulbright Program, accessed May 10, 2020.

Serena discovered the program through a friend who had participated in the program herself. Her friend had the chance to study in Europe, and Serena feels inclined to apply to the same. If accepted, Serena's goal would be to go to Finland to discover aspects of her own heritage and continue her studies.

On the other hand, Serena really loves culture and lifestyle journalism. One of her favorite things to do is to listen to people talk and tell their stories. She has considered getting a job where she can cover profiles. The post-grad lane is wide open for Serena.

"I just love like listening to people's stories and like hearing about their lives and how they got where they are, whatever that looks like," Serena said.

Serena finds that food criticism is a very niche field, and her passion has expanded to enjoying writing about culture, trends, travel, food, and profiles. Her passion for storytelling has the chance to lead her in many different directions. Realistically, the college student aims to work at a magazine so she can work on long feature stories and narratives or work on graphics and edit pieces.

"I love print journalism, but I'm also not opposed at all to online journalism. Either online magazines or companies like *Iridescent*," Serena revealed. "My three favorite things are food criticism, profiles, and culture. Anything in those realms is where I would hope to go, but we shall see."

This may sound slightly chaotic, but Serena is heading down a path that will lead her to toward her passions and subjects that make her happy. The journalism industry's fantastic thing is that things are always evolving, but they also simultaneously stay the same. Basic storytelling won't change, and there will always be more to learn and reveal. Serena could join the Fulbright program or get a job as a lifestyle writer. She has personal goals to guide her, and her path will play out as she goes. No one's path is the same, and I am very excited to see where she's going.

Serena is an easy gal to love. Her warmness invites you in, and her smile makes you feel at home. She truly has a heart for others, and it shows in her everyday life. When I asked her what advice she'd pass along to her younger self, she said she couldn't help herself and had to quote Cinderella.

"Have courage and be kind," Serena recalled. "Honestly, in the journalism world, you really need to be courageous and have valor because you're talking to strangers. You just have to put yourself out there or you're not going to get anywhere. People respond so well when you're kind to them."

I value Serena's story and insights because she is still figuring things out. She shows how not every path into the industry is the same, and everyone will have individually unique journeys. She has kept herself open to new opportunities and put herself out there, and she is making the most of it. Whether it is reaching out to a source or applying for a dream job, be courageous in your life every day. Just think about how twenty seconds of insane courage can lead to a decision that changes our lives—or others.

"If journalists have a chance to save their lives," Marie Colvin once said, "they should do so."[49]

Whether we are reporting from a war zone or covering conflict at the local city hall, our storytelling has the power to move people.

---

49 "Marie's Story," Marie Colvin Memorial Foundation, accessed October 1, 2020.

CHAPTER NINE

BE CURIOUS

Hello, my name is Lauren, and I'm a living, breathing spoiler alert.

Hi, Lauren.

Remind yourself never to invite me to watch a movie with you. Because I would accept the invitation, sit next to you, eat your popcorn and—for a while, at least—appear to be a perfectly normal moviegoer. Invariably, however, the plot would thicken. And I, invariably, would begin to get worked up and anxious about how the story might end.

I do realize that for most people, part of the joy of watching a film lies in not knowing how the arc of the story wraps around and ties like a tidy bow at the end. I'm just not one of those people. I love to get tangled up in suspended disbelief, but what I love more is to release it when my nerves can't take it anymore. I pull out my phone in the darkened cinema and let my curiosity absolutely get the best of me.

Hey, Siri. Did Marta give Harlan the wrong medicine in Knives Out on purpose?

It's a wonder anyone will watch a movie with me, but I just can't help myself sometimes. When I know the ending,

I can watch the rest of the movie with an informed perspective that illuminates nuances, subtleties, and hints of what's to come. I have a curiosity to know to look for those details. While our curiosity can sometimes lead to spoilers, it can also give us answers we need.

Innovation and invention come from the inquisitive minds of those of us who actively let our curiosity get the best of us. When we allow ourselves to follow it, curiosity often leads us to people who offer insight. *Glamour* Editor-in-Chief Samantha Berry is one of those people. *Glamour* is an online magazine housed under the umbrella of Condé Nast Publications and focuses on covering women's issues and stories authentically.[50] One of my favorite events they host is the Glamour Women of the Year Awards. During the awards, they honor "game changers, rule breakers, and trailblazers."[51] I dream of attending the award show one day. Can you imagine being surrounded by such amazing women? *Whew, the power the room would exude.*

I have a massive journalism crush on Berry. *Can we make that a thing?* She may not be a household name yet like Anna Wintour, but she is working to take her magazine into the digital age with a significant focus on keeping content honest and truthful. If I were granted an opportunity to meet any current editor-in-chief I wanted to, I would pick Berry.

Berry did a quick interview with FLIK, a community platform for ambitious women to connect with each other, in November 2019. The company's mission is to help female leaders grow their businesses through resources, mentors,

---

50 "Glamour," Condé Nast, accessed October 1, 2020.
51 "Women of the Year," Glamour, accessed October 1, 2020.

and new opportunities.[52] Berry noted how she got to see a lot of the world early in her career, and how she has always been "appreciative of other people's cultures."[53] She is a classic storyteller who wants to discover the hidden stories around the world.

"I have always been curious about other people's stories," Berry said. "I think that really helps you as a journalist, as an editor, as a reporter."[54]

Journalists are always telling a story and are consistently searching for a way to inform people. To be a journalist, we need to be curious. Curiosity leads to questions, and when questions lead to answers, we now have something to share with the world. This is what has taken Berry's career to the next level and is a principle to laying down a foundation for journalists. Stories begin with questions to be asked, and questions are formed from curiosities about the world.

Christiana Nielson graduated from the University of Missouri-Columbia in 2012 with a degree in magazine journalism and international studies. After she graduated, she went to work as an associate editor for the *Celebrated Living Magazine*, the first class and business class in-flight publication for American Airlines. As an associate editor, she covered the glitz and glamour of air travel. She then switched over to be an associate editor for *American Way*, the airline's other publication. As an associate editor for *American Way*, she got to edit pieces about entertainment, movies, books, and music.

When US Airways and American Airlines merged, the magazine ended up outsourced through a couple different

---

52 "Mission," FLIK, accessed October 1, 2020.
53 *The Leading Ladies at FLIK*, "5 Chapters w/ Samantha Barry (Editor-in-Chief of Glamour)," November 6, 2019, video, 7:03.
54 *The Leading Ladies at FLIK*, "5 Chapters w/ Samantha Barry."

hands. Leaving a wide-open door for her, Christiana left to join D *Magazine* in 2015 as the managing editor until she was laid off in March 2020 due to the pandemic. Christiana spent some time freelancing before joining the *D Magazine*'s content marketing agency, D Custom, as the managing editor.

Christiana is a self-starter and hard worker who has gone through some trial and errors to find what she loves and end up where she is today. If she has never stopped doing one thing, it is asking as many questions as she'd like.

Understand Your Skillset

Managing editors have to have a unique set of skills to be successful in their position. They are balancing different sections and people while trying to pull a magazine issue together. Someone who fits the role very well is Christiana.

From a young age, Christiana had a love for writing and editing. Before long, she also discovered her tendency to be very detailed and immensely organized. *Trust me, I watched it firsthand*. When I worked as her intern, I would see her work around her desk and laptop, and I dream of having my desktop that clean. Her computer is organized impeccably, and I would gladly pay her to organize my life—*I mean computer*.

She really liked what the managing editor position entailed: coordinating deadlines, deciding on content substitutions when needed, planning for the next issue, managing people, and still writing your own pieces. This is why she decided to apply for the opening at *D Magazine* in 2015, and she went into it with a level of confidence. She had developed the needed skills throughout her career and decoded to take a shot at applying for the role.

"You know, at first, I think I was a bit uncomfortable with it and you know, telling people what to do at twenty-five," Christiana reflected. "A year in I was like, well, it is what it is. As long as you're confident and know what you're doing, people are going to respect you even if you're young."

Christiana also supervised the magazine's editorial interns, managed logistics and shipping, and liaised between the editorial and art production departments. She managed special projects like the medical directory and had her own writing included in issues. Writing is truly at the core of it all for Christiana, and she knew she wanted to keep it that way with her role.

"A lot of writers do not have the sort of organizational, like detailed, managerial part as well," Christiana commented. "They're just very creative. I was drawn to both and so that's what I liked about it. I liked having my hand in, you know, a part of everything."

Be a Self-Starter

Landing jobs and internships can be challenging, whether we are in school or post-grad. The market is competitive, and when we do find ones to apply to, we are continually battling with different amounts of people to land the role. We can have as little or as much as we want on our resume, but it's all about what we can offer a company. It's how we can prove we are the ones for the job. Getting the first foot in the industry's door can be challenging, but sometimes it takes the right connection, the right place at the right time, or the right mindset to land it. It's all about getting started and the first foot through the door.

"I feel like once you do that and you have things on your resume, it's easier," Christiana said. "And you have connections."

People looking to hire may be willing to bypass the lack of experience or skills needed when we appear hardworking and eager to learn. Internships and jobs are meant to be teaching positions and areas for growth, so it's essential to make your curiosity to expand your knowledge clear.

When Christiana realized her writing strong suit came naturally as a teenager, she joined the newspaper staff at school. Christiana had no problem getting herself out into the world to share a story. Her ambition did not know limits, and she sent letters to the editor at the *Dallas Morning News* as an attempt to get her stuff published while still in high school.

"I was kind of obsessed," Christiana reflected. "I feel like I just loved getting to craft people's stories in a way that would be engaging."

This craftiness is what caught the attention of Tim Rogers at *D Magazine* early on in her career. She had no managing editor experience at all, but he could see the potential behind her eagerness to ask questions and discover more. Christiana's mindset pushes herself—and others—to find the best content and create something important to people. Now, she gets to look for those same characteristics in younger journalists.

Everyone has to start somewhere. There will be someone who sees the greatness within and will want to give us a chance to set everything in motion. I know I've had someone like this at each point in my career: Nicole giving me my first internship, Christiana helping me get my first published piece, and Eric Koester for reaching out and encouraging me to write this book.

Christiana knows what it's like on both ends and now has extensive experience in picking out interns. She examined the hopeful resumes, conducted the nerve-racking interviews, and has been the person to offer a new opportunity for someone.

She found it fun to help coach and teach her interns at *D Magazine*. Christiana looked for the go-getters and proactive interns when hiring. Writing skills are important, but it is a skill that can be worked on and developed over time. Team players and self-starters were essential qualities needed. Those are the things more difficult to teach and develop when it doesn't come naturally. For example: she wouldn't want to hire someone that she has to keep reminding to do their work or to come up with stories.

"You can't always tell," Christiana said. "But, it's usually pretty clear the people who are going to sort of take it and run with it."

Be the applicant that is ready to learn. Nothing is wrong with being humble enough to admit that we don't have all the skills needed, and we can still be confident when we do this. We can believe in ourselves but still want to expand our knowledge. Be the one curious about the world.

(You Should) Love What You Do

While in college, Christiana dipped her toe into the newspapers and magazine waters to see which medium she preferred. She gravitated toward the flexible style of magazines and the important voice within prolonged, feature pieces. The emphasis on people and human interests pulled her in that direction. Within magazines, Christiana found more room to express herself with the writing and more space to do it well.

"It's not the easiest field to be in," Christiana commented. "It's not like you're always going to have job security or make a million dollars, but it's really fun. I feel like a lot of importance has to do with doing what makes you happy and what you love as well. I've always loved reading magazines growing up. It's really artistic. Newspaper doesn't have that sort of design element either."

There's a good ole saying that fits well with this: "Choose a career you love and you will never have to go to work." Passion is at the core of everything we do. We don't simply choose to write because we think it's what we should do—it's what we want to do. If we can narrow what kind of storyteller we are, then we will find fulfillment and a drive to keep doing it.

Use Trial and Error

We can start from the baseline of our skills and build up. Interests can turn into passions, and layers of skills can be added on top of it. Within the industry, some are made to be writers, some are better suited as editors, and some are better off having Grammarly installed on every device.

The industry is full of unique roles and positions, but the core of it all is storytelling. A team will be built of different personalities and skills to be well-rounded enough to tell an impactful story. Roles with singular focuses do not mean we are not good at other things, but rather, it means that we can shine in one part so someone else can shine in theirs. **It's okay to not be the best at everything.** What unites everyone together is their love for informing people and telling stories;

we just have to use our drive and curiosity to discover which way we do it best. Not everyone's path to this enlightenment will look the same either.

"If you want to find out people's stories and share them, you're going to be able to do that no matter what your degree is in," Christiana stated. "People don't have to go to journalism school to be a journalist. I happened to go that route… You don't have to have a journalist background to be a journalist."

We can't give up when we get rejected, we just have to keep trying. Keep sending those introduction emails and informational interview requests. When we finally get the opportunity to learn from someone, then the world is at our feet, waiting to be discovered. Christiana commented that "journalism is something you learn more by doing," and I could not agree more. If we keep trying out new things, then we will stumble across the thing that lights a fire inside and screams, "this was made for me."

"I had some friends in college find out that it just really wasn't for them and not everybody wants to stick it out," Christiana said. "I feel like just starting to talk to people and write. Write about things you're interested in… I think talking to people who have it made it their career is really probably a good place to start."

Many people shaped their careers by being curious and asking questions. In her own words, Christiana is a person who "asks unending questions to an annoying point." She has a desire to know the point of everything. It can be a story, a book, or a movie—anything. Her nature is to be curious about the world.

To her, being curious is the first step to showing that we care to tell people's stories to other people. We have to want within to find out more—to find out more about the local city council meeting, or how a person started a million-dollar company from scratch. Be open-minded and let your curious mind wonder what you can discover and cover next. Ask the deep questions that go beyond the surface level of a story. Great narratives are written with the information we find when we go deeper than what someone wants us to see, but we won't get to craft those great stories if we leave our curiosity at the door.

"You don't have to be an expert in every single thing to write about it. You just have to be willing to learn and do the research and talk to experts," Christiana stated.

Christiana's curiosity for the world is what led her to double major in college. She carefully planned her classes to study both journalism and international studies and fueled her passion for different cultures while learning how to become a great journalist. Christiana's interest in broadening her knowledge about the world led to a studying abroad stint in London, and she flourished a passion for researching different cultures that exist outside of the United States.

Her international studies background improved her skills as a journalist when traveling and writing because it expanded her awareness of how other cultures differ. As of April 2020, Christiana has traveled to around twenty-one different countries with plans to visit Peru and Africa. The trips were canceled due to the pandemic, but she still hopes to visit one day.

I don't think her curiosity and drive to travel will ever fade. The seasoned traveler sees London's streets and rainy weather as a second home, and some of her favorite memories come from a trip she took to Argentina with her sister. She got to enjoy everything from wine tastings to learning more about the country's culture.

"I feel like I have so many good memories from traveling," Christiana commented. "I've traveled to most, at least, Western European countries, too. Those are some great memories that I have. But Argentina was awesome."

Christiana's appreciation for the world inspires me and reminds me to keep my fire of curiosity alive—to let it guide me toward stories and new opportunities. I've always told people they cannot tell me something and not expect me to ask more questions. I simply have to know more. Be the annoying person asking all the questions and don't stop until answers have been given. Then share it with the world.

CHAPTER TEN

BE CONFIDENT

Every couple of years, my family and I road trip to New Mexico during the holiday season. In Dallas, the weather will be in the 70s and sunny. By the time we hit the border between the states, the temperature will have dropped massively, and if we are lucky, we see our first sights of snow. The twelve-hour trip always runs smoothly, as my parents are confident in our route, the rotated tires, and how long it will take us to arrive at our destination.

Laying down a strong foundation is vital when it comes to the construction of different infrastructures. A highway is a particular path created to take people from one end to another. If the foundations are shaky, then the possibilities of people making it from one end to another would decrease. Who wants to go on a road unsure if it will be safe for them?

Similarly, the infrastructure for our journey to success is built upon our self-confidence. Like an overpass with crumbling support, if we don't have a stable belief of confidence in ourselves, small comments can quickly bring us down. To create the framework of our confidence we must first lay down a secure foundation of confidence, then build upon it.

Why is confidence important? Confidence is believing in your own capabilities and feeling assured of what you accomplish. It's trust and reliability, and to make it in the journalism industry, we need it within ourselves.

In 2016, City, University of London hosted a Women on Air panel to discuss the importance of confidence and mentoring in the journalism industry. Fatima Manji, a United Kingdom-based Channel 4 News correspondent, agreed with other panelists that female journalists bring something unique to the news.

"Whether it's pushing back on a story or walking in and saying, 'I want to be on that story,' I think [confidence] is what's changed on an individual level," Manji said.[55]

We're not born with self-confidence. If we're lucky, we have parents and caregivers who help to instill it within us in early childhood. But most of us spend the rest of our lives building our sense of self and rebuilding it when our shortcomings cause self-doubt to creep in and whisper into our ears. When you hear the voice of doubt—whether it's that of an internal or external critic—speak up. "I can do this." Instead of dwelling on what you think you *should* be, open up to the possibilities of what you *could* be.

Make a path where there is none, or around obstacles standing in the way. Conquer the paths the naysayers think is impossible. No one else can strut down our paths in the way we can. Like every great highway being built, we have the opportunity to lay down each pillar and watch a beautiful connection be created. It will change as our lives do, but it is never too late to make confident decisions to clear the way for us.

---

55 Mădălina Ciobanu, "'Women on air' discuss the importance of confidence and mentoring to succeed in the media industry," *Journalism.co.uk*, June 1, 2016.

Melissa Shook is the founder and publisher of the Dallas-Fort Worth wedding magazine *The Southern Social*. The Texan launched the magazine in 2018 after a ten-year *(yes, I said ten)* career as a wedding photographer in the metroplex before deciding to change her career path. Her transformation from wedding photographer to magazine owner flourished through a combination of confidence and passion for weddings.

When we met, Melissa owned a photography business in my hometown. She had created a unique "senior team" to promote senior photo sessions. We did fun things like styled shoots and discounted senior photos *(my parents enjoyed that part)*. A fellow classmate and I did a '50s and '60s vintaged-themed styled shoot at a local restaurant, Farm Luck, for one of the styled photoshoots. Melissa had a clear eye for how to pull everything together for the retro-themed photoshoot.

On the morning of the shoot, I showed up early, ready to be dolled up. I often feel awkward in front of the camera. *You should see me trying to take simple Instagram photos.* Melissa made me feel comfortable and confident while taking my picture. She has a creative eye for envisioning styled shoots and an ability to connect with people quite easily.

Her gravitation toward the wedding industry started with her admiration for weddings as she spent countless hours observing weddings through the lens of a camera. Melissa's photography business helped her learn to communicate with couples. Melissa **loves** love.

"Weddings were my passion," Melissa reflected. "I loved shooting weddings. I know that's a little cliche and everybody says it, but it was a lot of fun for me."

She began to pull away from her photography business when she realized what the time commitment kept her from. Melissa is a mom to two children and would often be working on weekends. Her moment of realization occurred on her way to shoot a wedding on a Saturday. She missed her son's first pee-wee football game to go shoot the wedding. Melissa's love for weddings did not come before her role as a mother. She cried the whole way to the wedding because she missed a significant milestone in her child's life.

"I know it's pee-wee football, but I was missing it," Melissa commented. "That was kind of the point where I was like, 'I want my weekends back. I love photography, but this isn't really working for me anymore.'"

Melissa then decided to start her mission of finding a new opportunity to give her some freedom back. Melissa knew it wasn't in her cards to go back to what some may consider a "real" job; working for someone else after owning her own photography business affected this. She knew she wanted to work for herself and do what she wanted to do, so Melissa created her own opportunity.

Melissa had become very comfortable and well-versed in the wedding industry at that point. With her industry topic chosen, she then had to figure out what she could create from it. She considered her own capabilities and what lacked from the metroplex wedding industry market. It all became evident at that point.

Melissa recalled saying that at that moment, "Hey, I could do a magazine, can't I?"

A magazine production schedule allows her to work through the week and spend much-needed time with her children on the weekends. She can control her own time. *Oh, and be her own boss still. Mission accomplished.*

Melissa started with the basics. She knew she could utilize her own background in graphic design. The goal centered around creating an eye-catching magazine design for the modern bride. Melissa knew she had enough knowledge in how weddings came together but had to figure out how to produce a magazine with no journalistic or production experience.

She based her research goal on determining what goes into making a magazine: the procedure for the physical production of a print magazine, any costs, and what she needed to include in the issues. Melissa says she, oddly enough, does not remember actually starting the magazine. Everything went by in a blur for her, and when *The Southern Social* launched in 2018, she never looked back.

"Honestly I don't remember actually starting it," Melissa reflected. "I just remember it happening. That whole first part was just a blur to me. I just did it. No questions asked, [I] just figured it out myself and did it."

The Dallas-Fort Worth metroplex has a few notable wedding publications (*D Weddings, 360 West Magazine, Brides of North Texas*), but Melissa saw an opportunity for a different type of print wedding magazine. Melissa approached her brainstorming sessions intending to find the next trend to put a twist on and make her own. She thought about how she could offer the most for her consumers. She came up with *The Southern Social*, a magazine aimed at educating couples planning a wedding rather than just telling them what to do. She wanted to create a mutual relationship with couples where they feel like they're learning and not just repeating what was said to them. Melissa wanted to improve the experience for her readers.

"I tell people all the time [that] I'm not reinventing the wheel with what we're doing. We're just trying to do it in a different way that it nobody else has done before," Melissa said. "My mind is always going like, 'How can I make this better? How can we make this different?'"

Melissa and *The Southern Social* are always looking to introduce new ideas and vendors to their customers. The team has to have a unique strategy. Most customers will use them to plan their wedding but then lose interest once they have their event. Melissa had to consider how to grow revenues, build a loyal fanbase, gain trust for advertisements, and encourage continuous recommendations.

Be Passionate and Make It Happen

Melissa had the background needed to establish her own magazine from photography business experience but didn't quite have the editorial knowledge. She knew she had her passion for weddings and decided her confidence would lead her in the right direction—and the best team.

"I'm not a journalist, I'm not a writer," Melissa said. "I'm none of those things. But Google does some wonderful things for you."

Melissa never doubted her ability to create a successful print magazine when she began developing the first issue of *The Southern Social*. Her lack of sales experience didn't stop her from selling the idea of the magazine to people. Melissa confidently pitched the idea to the connections she already had and found herself with enough content, photographs, and article submissions to launch her first issue. Her confidence in constructing the magazine shone bright because of her passion for weddings. If Melissa wanted to put out a magazine, she would do it one way or another.

Melissa believed in her magazine's mission and refused to let any industry standards get in her way of publishing her print magazine. *I cannot imagine what it is like to tell people you are launching a magazine without the editorial experience in your back pocket.* When women like Melissa decide to break past the barriers standing in the way of their end goal, I find myself extremely inspired. She intends to live life to the fullest. The combination of passion, confidence, and good intentions is a hard combo for people to ignore.

The confidence Melissa radiates from within herself attracts people to her. Melissa often has people reaching out to her (*which she loves*) to do some freelance work for the magazine and questions about how she started from scratch. She keeps these people in mind when there are new opportunities. Melissa understands the pressure that starting from the beginning and then defying the odds set out against you can cause. If she let all the thoughts and feedback get further ahead in a race against her confidence, then she would never see her full vision come to life.

"It's okay if you fail. You might not fail at the whole thing, but there might be pieces that don't fall together," Shook commented. "I'm tired of caring about what anybody else thinks or does. I know that this is what I'm doing; [this is] my vision for what I'm trying to create."

Melissa's saving grace came from shutting out any negativity from others throughout the process of launching her magazine. Her confidence helped her trust her gut, and in return, put her energy into what she is creating. We have to make the conscious decision to be confident whenever we are starting something new. If we don't believe in what we are producing, then how can we expect others to? Put your passionate energy out in the world and see how beautiful life can be.

Be a Team Player

While she pulled together the first magazine issue with the help of contributors, Melissa slowly formed her staff. As of spring 2020, *The Southern Social* team included a senior editor/content writer, a social media manager, a style director, and another contributing writer and editor. Melissa's lack of a journalism degree doesn't stand between her and overseeing the team, design, and content. Melissa knew what she wanted to handle within the magazine, so her search for a team revolved around filling in the gaps.

"I do a little bit of everything," Melissa reflected. "But we're growing. I'm trying to add a good team to kind of help do the other stuff that I don't want to. My love and passion is the magazine and the design."

Local journalism student Abbie Mckelvey joined Melissa first after meeting through a class called "Leadership Midlothian." *Remember what I said about Melissa's confident energy bringing in similar minds?* Abbie approached Melissa and asked to get coffee after hearing a presentation done by Melissa. *A bold move.* During their first meeting, Abbie told Melissa she had always wanted to work for a magazine, so Melissa offered her internship. Abbie played a crucial part in the beginning of *The Southern Social* until distance caused her to leave the team behind.

"I love her to death," Melissa said. "That kind of just fell into my lap. I wasn't really looking for anything, but that happened." As *The Southern Social* grew, Melissa eventually added her social media manager, style director, social rep, graphic design intern, and other additional contributing writers.

"We do things a little differently," Melissa said. "We have what we call our round tables. I'm a team player. I'll pitch ideas, like 'Hey, this is what I want to see in the next issue,' or 'These are some ideas.' Then we all just kind of talk and go through some things."

The Southern Social is successful with the team surrounding Melissa. Everyone can use any energy bouncing off of each other to produce something they are all proud of, highlighting their unique talents. Melissa may lead the pack, but she does not control it. The level of trust between the small team flourishes into something special.

Everyone has to be willing to give their all to the team and mission for it to be successful, and when this kind of energy is put off, it will attract people to the magazine. Be passionate about what you are doing, be confident when it is published, and be ready for people to read it.

Connections are Vital

Connections are a vital part of the success of *The Southern Social*. Melissa built up relationships with different business over the years through her contacts in the wedding industry as a photographer.

Melissa brainstormed early on how to build up trust between her and the people supporting the magazine. She had to find a way to make money and still offer the best content to their readers. The sweet middle spot between these two aspects created the "featured pros" aspect of *The Southern Social*. The missing advertising spots were filled with featured professionals from the industry to advertise their products. To solidify this idea, Melissa chose to reach out to her network to get connections started.

Some of the first featured pro vendors were from Melissa's specific list of company connections she has built upon over the years. Vendors are the magazine's advertisers, and they give these businesses a chance to educate potential clients. It's an opportunity for brands to showcase their field and section of the industry. Melissa created such a foundational part of the magazine (*and its revenues*) through her previous connections. Every issue is a collaboration between the team and vendors.

If we are always on the lookout for new opportunities and are willing to put ourselves out there, we will be surprised at what connections we make. Don't second guess yourself, own what you are doing, and be open to failure. People want to help us and be in community with us. Whether it is on LinkedIn or within an office, our connections can lead us to a multitude of opportunities.

Find the Thing That Sets You Apart

Melissa knew when she created her magazine that she had to find a way to set it apart from others. She saw an opening for a new print publication within the DFW area, even with how many blogs and websites are available as resources for weddings on the internet. Melissa does not think print journalism is dying.

"I don't think print's dead," Melissa commented. "I don't think print will ever be dead. I love magazines. I think magazines are really, really cool and I think a lot of people really do like them."

The Southern Social, as an independently owned and produced magazine, releases two issues each year. You can find print copies within the featured pros' offices or homes, select Kendra Scott locations, and various venue open houses.[56]

Melissa stayed adamant that she would not release just any old magazine. She wanted it to be different—for it to stand out from the others. Melissa found her uniqueness within the industry with how she handles the advertisement portion of the magazine. Melissa sought to eliminate the pages of traditional advertisements to reach a modern audience. Vendors, which would be your typical advertisers, have a distinct purpose within the magazine and its direction. They can customize their involvement in the issues and present their business in an aesthetically appealing way to educate the reader and promote their product.

Vendors create content, the editors write about what is going on, and the overall goal is to educate the reader. This can be an article essentially sponsored by a vendor. If you opened up a magazine issue, you would not find your typical advertisement pages. *The Southern Social* seeks to present this information usefully and tries to be honest about prices. The different magazine issues help educate readers about how much a wedding actually costs, which is not something all wedding magazines do. There is a range of vendors and styles.

The magazine's goal of changing the way couples can plan and find their vendors is impactful its own way. Watching Melissa's journey with *The Southern Social* from afar has inspired me as someone who always dreamed of launching their own magazine. A barrier of doubt is removed from my mind by watching Melissa pull off her launch and success.

We don't have to have all the necessary skills life pushes us to do what we want. She helped put down a footprint

---

56 "FAQ," The Southern Social, accessed June 18, 2020.

in the path for people who dream but maybe do not have the background. If we believe in ourselves, then why should anyone have doubts?

One of the dreamers Melissa is inspiring daily is her own daughter, Harper. Now a full-fledged teenager *(she turned thirteen during the 2020 pandemic)*, she has been asking her Mom when she gets to be in the magazine herself. That is just the beginning of her long-term relationship with her Mom's magazine.

"She says one day she's going to take over the magazine and she's going to run it," Melissa commented. "Which I'm all for."

Whether it's her daughter, me, or the next wedding magazine extraordinaire, Melissa's advice is simple: dream big and go big. Anything can be possible if we are willing to work hard for it. People listen when confidence and passion speak through us. We will attract the energy we put out, so why not choose to be assertive in that decision? Melissa built up her confidence over the years and decided to take a bet on herself with no insurance of success. Are you ready to start promoting your own confidence without feeling any doubt or without feeling guilty?

CHAPTER ELEVEN

BE VALUABLE

Katie Couric has never been one to check her initiative at the door.

Fresh out of college, a young, bright-eyed Katie Couric worked as a desk assistant for ABC News in Washington. While there, she took the initiative to pitch eight story ideas to then-20/20 anchor Don Farmer. Farmer, impressed with her confidence, remembered Katie when he moved to CNN and needed a producer for his new show.[57] *A full circle.*

"Be willing to work hard, work long hours, and be the person where they say, 'We need someone this weekend to do something,' and be an eager beaver," Katie stated. "You have to get there; you have to be willing to do a lot of things. People really do notice when you have initiative and you go above and beyond what's expected of you. I don't think people realize that just a little, some small things are often, you know, noticed, and they do make a difference."[58]

---

57 *CBS News*, "Katie's advice for aspiring journalists," February 25, 2011, video, 4:31.
58 *CBS News*, "Katie's advice for aspiring journalists."

Katie graduated with a degree in American studies from the University of Virginia. In 1991, she started her fifteen-year journey as a host of The Today Show for NBC News. Spending five weekday mornings in millions of American living rooms each week quickly made her a household name. But Katie Couric was far from finished making a name for herself. When she joined CBS Evening News, she became the first woman to solo anchor a network evening newscast.[59] When she left the CBS news desk, she did some special event reporting for ABC News and executive produced two documentaries, *Fed Up* and *Gender Revolution: A Journey with Katie Couric*.[60] Finally, In 2017, Katie founded her namesake media company. Katie Couric Media has developed several media projects, including a daily newsletter, a podcast, a digital video series, and several documentaries. Is there any wonder why she has twice been listed among *Time's* 100 Most Influential People?[61]

Throughout her career, Katie has been a prolific creator of content, and that has been a critical component of success for the three-time *Glamour Magazine* Woman of the Year.

"The more you write," Katie said, "the more you interview people, the more stories you do… the better you are going to be."[62]

By continuing to develop and refine our craft, we can build our value in an ever-changing media landscape and, like Katie, be ready to adapt to it.

To gain another valuable view, I talked to someone who is learning to be adaptable starting off in their career. For

---

59 "About Katie Couric," Katie Couric Media, accessed October 26, 2020.
60 "Katie Couric," LinkedIn, accessed June 21, 2020.
61 "About KCM," Katie Couric Media, accessed June 21, 2020.
62 *CBS News*, "Katie's advice for aspiring journalists."

privacy reasons, she requested that I refer to her as Jane. After graduating from an Ivy League school in 2017, Jane started as a full-time reporter in 2018.

A passion for storytelling motivated Jane as a teenager. She wrote fantasy books as a kid, so naturally, she decided to start writing for her high school paper. Jane jumped straight into reporting about school plays, teachers' journeys, new school programs, and—as she put it—"really, really small town stuff." Jane escaped the "small town stuff" to attend an Ivy League school, where she studied American studies in material cultures and built environments.

While not the expected journalism major, she moved toward her passion. Her choice of a major was not the end of her writing career, though. While she may have been super passionate about cultural aspects and environment choices, she still had an eye for developing her writing skills. Jane received a copy of her new college's weekly newspaper's special edition issue and decided to take a chance on it.

"I remember just being so excited by how funny it was, how smart it was, and thinking like, 'I want to be a part of this,'" Jane reflected.

She would go on to not only join her college's different assortment of publications, but would be the editor-in-chief of the paper at one point. She found herself drawn to using storytelling to elevate the voices sharing real stories to influence people in their city. *Quite the mission, if you ask me.* Her interest peaked when looking beyond the normal aspects of her college town and looking beyond the bubble around her to see how the city operated as an overall ecosystem.

"That's what got me interested in writing about cities and the people that live in them," Jane commented.

Jane gravitated toward urban policy and political science over her college years. Her passion for writing about cities grew throughout her time in college as a staff writer, culture editor, managing editor, executive editor, and editor-in-chief of the weekly newspaper over the years. She also helped launch a new, independent literary and travel magazine as an editorial assistant with different audio readings, articles, web content, and a weekly newsletter that she managed.

Before she completed her time at her Ivy League college, she worked as a senior editor for her school's magazine. But she also worked as a research assistant for the New York University Robert F. Wagner Graduate School of Public Service. As a research assistant, she looked at the connection between housing quality and public health.

Step Out of Comfort Zones

After graduating, Jane ended up with an internship at a popular online media-political site based in Virginia *(for privacy concerns, I am not going to name the specific places Jane has worked at)*. Her internship happened to be during President Trump's first summer in office, an experience she described as "really instructive."

"[I] got to go outside of my comfort zone to do some national political reporting to figure out what was up with nuclear deterrence in Korea, to really intense fact-checking in a magazine process," Jane said. "I wasn't really familiar with [it] so that was a really great learning experience."

Jane took this time to figure out where she wanted her reporting to lean more toward. Stepping out of her comfort zone and tackling important issues became essential. After her internship, she considered that maybe she still had an interest in local communities rather than national. Jane even found herself pulled toward how innovation can happen on a city level and its impact on the community.

She felt like she underappreciated her previous work. A sense of obligation to report on local community events, right in their backyard, became her new focus. This kind of work could have national implications. Stepping out of her comfort zone that summer guided Jane toward her preferred subject to report on: cities.

Sometimes we find ourselves so locked in on the thing we *think* we are supposed to write about that we don't see what we *can* write on. If we are passionate about a subject, it never hurts to step out of our comfort zone to report something unknown to us to gain clarity on it.

Find Ways to Grow

Whether you're in college, post-grad, or mid-career, finding a new way to grow can never hurt. As humans, we are always evolving. And we can experience plenty of moments of feeling lost when exploring new opportunities.

When young journalists graduate from college or step into a new aspect of their life, they often feel lost and unsure where to go; they can get internships, choose to get their master's, get a job, or join a fellowship. A fellowship is a program for post-grad students and is very common for many journalists looking for a way into the industry. As a fellow, you can be in a weird limbo of not being classified as an intern but not being a full-fledged staff member. This is the route Jane took.

"I did the fellowship, which was a really great early career experience," Jane commented. "[I] learned a lot from my fellow fellows. What was cool about the editorial fellowship was that they gave you a lot of responsibility. It was definitely a learning experience."

Fellowships are great for the experience, but not for the pay. Fellows will be paid more than an intern, but less than a staff member. For someone living in a larger city for the position, the budget can be tight. Jane says there need to be more meaningful conversations and transparency on what fellows have to be successful without money limitations. It's not the path for everyone, and Jane hopes fellows will start to see a raise in wages to match their hard work.

Jane thinks a fellowship is great for on-the-ground learning experiences. During her fellowship, her team she treated her like a full-time employee. The company offered Jane a full-time job at the end of her fellowship—a transition she didn't find difficult. Jane felt like a staff writer during her experience, and she loved the team. She found it exciting to kick off her professional writing and reporting career at the media company. Sadly, not everyone has that opportunity when they finish their fellowship.

"It's such a crap shoot kind of, like whether you get a job at the end of it, [even] if you work hard," Jane said. "There's just not enough jobs in journalism. If you do a good job of the fellowship, you're not automatically going to get a full-time offer from the company that's giving you a fellowship. So I think that's another important thing to remember."

Establish Your Expertise

Jane believes her previous work set her up to land jobs and internships. When applying to jobs and internships, we want our resume to be the one employers pull out of a pile. Jane would recommend establishing our expertise and specific interest in a subject or two. It isn't about knowing everything, but knowing what we want to grow and learn in.

"I think emphasizing how your research, and your college path or your personal experience, informs a very specific perspective and subject matter focus in your writing really helps," Jane commented.

If we are the best reporters to write about a specific topic, then we have to establish that. Making this known shows that we care about what we are writing about. Editors are looking for the people that are going to get the job done. We have to start presenting ourselves as experts and showing the value we can bring.

Remember the Value of Journalism

Jane currently works as a staff writer, reporting on local policy, housing, and technology in cities. Combining her love for cities and writing has allowed her to flourish as a journalist, but she says that she has to remember the privilege she has. She finds it amazing that she gets to be a journalist and tell people's stories.

"Especially during Coronavirus and during the current moment when people are so isolated and people are struggling so much... everyone is having such different experience of this one collective moment," Jane reflected. "I think I really remembered how amazing it is that I get to call people and ask them how they're doing and share their stories as honestly and as respectfully as I can."

Her advice to people looking to go into the industry, or anyone in it already, is to remember the responsibilities of journalism. When we feel ourselves getting jaded, stop and recognize the value of what you do and the importance (and coolness) of our job.

"I want to remember that for myself," Jane said. "I think social media and just the public-facing nature of the role is really stressful sometimes and [it can be] really scary to put yourself out there. Surrounding yourself with mentors and friends and people that can support you, that you trust to give you good advice, and talk you through hard times is really important too. It's really stressful to have to put your work out there and face people that might disagree with you or might like send you mean emails."

We are journalists who tell the world's stories. The meaning of our work can be blinded by people's emotions, social media, and stressful times. Keeping a great community around us can help remind us *why* we chose journalism in the first place. Remember to stay calm, breathe, and respond professionally. We got this!

People like Jane give me hope for the future of journalism. She also participates in a mentor program and has a heart for guiding the next generation of journalists.

"Be open to opportunities, even if they're not the ones that you originally thought you were qualified for, or you wanted to pursue," Jane said. "Because, especially when you're young and starting out writing about everything, being open to tackling a variety of kinds of stories and kinds of medias is super important. If someone offers you an opportunity to write a big magazine piece, like just say yes and figure it out. Um, don't burn out, don't over-stress yourself."

It's essential to be open to new opportunities and remember the other side of the coin. Journalism is a fast-paced, stressful industry. The job market is tough, and even when you have a job, it's tough watching your colleagues get sacked in round after round of layoffs, contract buy-outs, mergers, and closures. Remember to take time for yourself. We are much more valuable when we are our best selves, not some tired, overstressed version of ourselves. You are valuable because you are you, and no one else can replicate your voice. Separate that from your work as a reporter.

Stories are valuable because we are.

PART FOUR

WHAT TO DO NOW

CHAPTER TWELVE

FOR MY HIGH SCHOOL FRIENDS

No age minimum or limit exists for when you can speak up about the things that matter to us.

In November 2016, Berkeley High School senior Natalie Bettendorf spoke at a TEDx Talk event. Bettendorf, only eighteen at the time, helped manage her award-winning high school paper, the *Berkeley High Jacket,* while working at Youth Radio. During her time at Youth Radio, she had the chance to be featured on NPR's *All Things Considered* show and appeared as a guest on KQED Newsroom. The managing editor emphasized why youth journalism is vital for elevating the voices of young people.[63]

"Why is youth journalism important? Because it makes youth feel that their voices matter," Bettendorf commented. "Because they do. So when we have youth voices in journalism and telling stories, it actually helps you find your own voice."[64]

---

63 *Tedx Talks,* "Empowerment Through Youth Journalism | Natalie Bettendorf | TEDxYouth@EB," December 14, 2016, video, 15:15.
64 *Tedx Talks,* "Empowerment Through Youth Journalism."

To students with an interest in the field of journalism, Bettendorf recommends finding ways to incorporate news-gathering skills into daily life. Start by actively incorporating discrete practices: ask questions frequently, follow up on answers until subject comprehension is achieved, read everything from a newspaper to a cereal box, and be limitlessly curious about the world.[65] Begin thinking like a journalist and practice looking for moments to turn into a story. "You'll realize words have the power to make you feel any emotion in the world," Bettendorf said.[66]

Take Classes and Start Writing, Editing

One of my college professors told our class that "the world looks different after one hundred bylines." Why not get started as soon as possible?

If your school offers journalism or media classes, jump at the chance to learn the basics. Knowing how to format and structure an article will give you the framework for reporting on any topic or issue. Then you can begin to build your skills and hone your craft. Don't look at graded assignments as dreadful responsibilities, but rather creative opportunities.

If your school does not offer a media or journalism class, check to see if there's a school paper or yearbook staff to join. Your English teacher may know of other opportunities at school or in your community. Look for local writing workshops at the public library or community center. Sign up for a continuing education course at your local community college

---

65 Ibid.
66 Ibid.

or find a fun class online. Watch a webinar or a YouTube series. Reach out to a local reporter you admire and ask for suggestions. How you get your start isn't important, but you have to be determined to get started somewhere.

Developing skills over time requires writing, editing, and implementing feedback. Write, and write often. Write something every day if you can. And remember that every piece you write presents an opportunity to learn. It takes time to develop a knack for interviewing strangers, choosing the best quotes, recognizing credible facts and information, and weaving all of it together into a story that flows well. The more practice you get as an interviewer, researcher, and storyteller, the more skilled you'll become as a journalist.

Editing is another excellent tool for learning how to be a better writer. Whether you are editing your personal work or someone else's, you are learning as you go. As your mind fixes errors, it will make a mental note to not do the same thing again—*or at least try not to*. Your mind will become a natural editor.

Feedback can be critical when trying to grow as a writer. *Pardon my pun.* The first draft of anything isn't supposed to be perfect. It's a best first effort. Feedback is an editor's gift to help a journalist stretch and grow. If you're lucky enough to have someone who's willing to invest time and effort into offering feedback, then open your arms and accept that gift. It takes practice to learn to view negative feedback positively, but with that outlook, you'll grow far—as a journalist and as a human.

I will note that you must not feed your head with so much feedback that you lose your voice in whatever you write. Some people are just genuinely mean and quick to offer biting, unhelpful commentary. Teachers, mentors, and editors want to help us produce your best work. Funnel through any unnecessary, unwelcome commentary.

Once you have mastered the formulas and feedback, start getting your name out there. It is never too early to begin publishing your work correctly. If you focus on writing, getting bylines published where you can will play a significant role. If you concentrate on broadcast media, then any videos you can get on the Internet will also be crucial.

As your work improves over time, you will build up a list of articles that can help you apply for internships and college opportunities. High school articles can land journalism scholarships or a first internship in college. These pieces are vital in laying down a foundation as journalists. You will have your work in one hand and confidence in your writing in the other. The more you publish, the more confident you will be in your abilities.

Once you start publishing your work, you can start building up your portfolio. Online databases and portfolios have become an excellent option for young journalists to build up their brand from the start of their career. You can create a portfolio online that is eye-catching and covers you as a journalist as soon as you want. This will put you one step ahead because finding your work online and in one place will be easier. The start to building professional sides online can be fun, but you must remember that things stay on the Internet for a very long time. Think through things thoroughly and seek guidance if needed when creating a portfolio online. *If you have to question if it's appropriate, it probably isn't.*

Portfolios easily be created on websites like Wix, Squarespace, WordPress, or even Google Sites. You can make your websites for free, or choose an upgrade, to showcase your work as a journalist. If resources are available, buying a domain name is recommended *(for example, I bought laurenbannister.com for my portfolio)*.

Brainstorming is your first step. What do you want the theme to be? What fonts do you want to use? Any pictures you wish to include? Overall, how do you want to present yourself? Remember: this is not your diary. It is a portfolio that industry professionals can look at for scholarships, applications, and jobs. It looks very professional when you link a website for reference, and it makes it easier for people to get to learn more about you. The last thing needed is someone quickly exiting because your portfolio does not portray you correctly and looks unprofessional.

Portfolios are an easy storage system, but you should also save any work you want to keep just in case. Download PDFs of your work or print them if available. A certain heartbreak comes from databases and websites being removed with your work on it and having no way to find it. Gone forever. You don't want this to be a reality, as it's the baseline of your work as a journalist and a pillar of your resume—rather than it just floating around on the black hole of the Internet—you are going to want to have backups.

Jump at Opportunities for Camps, Conferences

I spoke briefly at the beginning of this book about my experiences at conferences, including ones at the University of Texas at Austin, the Mayborn Literary Nonfiction Conference, and the University of North Texas Mayborn School of Journalism High School Workshop. These experiences were crucial to my development as a high school journalist, from taking classes about journalism basics to interviewing established authors.

Unique camps can add a level of skills to your resume that a regular high school journalism class may not be able to. Camps and conferences are times for developing skills and networking. You can meet other high school journalists, but also industry professionals. Start researching for unique camp or workshop opportunities; high school advisors can also be great resources. Some camps and conferences potentially offer financial assistance as well.

When camps and conferences are not the best approach to learn, then you can hop onto YouTube to create a personal developmental skills camp. Get creative and find people who can offer you the same experience. The Internet is an excellent resource for research. Researching "journalism basics" can lead us to what the internet has to offer, and from there, building your own camp. Create a playlist on YouTube, start adding videos, and plan to sit down to enjoy them. Grab a notepad, a beverage, and get ready to learn.

When adding videos to a playlist, you need a variety of interviews with journalists, skill lessons, and published work to learn from. For example: an interview with legendary journalist Bob Woodward, a lesson on how to format a lede, and then an ABC Evening News piece. Round out the at-home conference with free online pdf readings, e-books, or available printed materials. You can do this alone or with a group of friends. The idea is to take the initiative to learn more and start homing in on your craft.

A good idea would also be to reach out to industry professionals, local or national. More often than not, journalists are willing to answer questions from young journalists and offer advice. They want to help you, and they want to leave an impact. Remember how powerful twenty seconds of courage can be. Draft a professional email or message for an industry professional and ask for a simple informational interview. Fifteen minutes with an industry professional can lead to hours of flourishing improvement for you.

Take Time for Your College Search

The college search process can be exciting and stressful.

I attended my first college fair as a sophomore to try and broaden understand what type of school would work best for me. I had gone into my freshman year knowing I wanted to go out of state, and for that to happen, I would need to find schools with scholarship programs.

Scholarships come in various sizes: school scholarships, sports scholarships, business scholarships, and more. My high school's counseling program had a running list of scholarship opportunities they kept available. To supplement the scholarships your high school finds, you can do your own research. Colleges offer a multitude of scholarships, grants, and financial aid. Start your research sooner rather than later as many scholarship deadlines occur in the fall time, and you don't want to miss out on getting your application in.

The vital thing to note here: college is about your education and not the school. Students tend to overlook small colleges and community colleges that offer a great education on a smaller scale and budget.

Given how new our journalism program is at my college, we have a small amount of people. We grow as journalists with each other through active class discussions and personal interactions. This is why research is so important. You can find a school best for you and work toward that end goal. The first college fair I went to had an interesting range of schools. Representatives ranged from Nottingham Trent University in England to the University of Missouri. As someone looking to study journalism, I focused in on locations and journalism programs.

Everyone's college search process will be different. I knew earlier on in high school that the University of Texas at Austin and the University of North Texas in Denton had great J-schools (journalism schools). Still, I had to consider what the schools offered all around. Starting my research early gave me time to compare and contrast my different options.

When you are looking at schools, I want you to consider two things: *major vs. minor* and *big fish vs. little fish*. If your goal is to major in journalism, then I recommend finding a school that offers it as a major. To me, this is what will be the best option and offer the most resources during your college years and post-grad. Some schools will offer a minor in journalism so that you can major in English or communications overall. If this is a route you want to take because you like the school or area, then that's the choice for you. If you're going to get involved in your college experience's journalism aspect, then finding a school with a *major* will be the best move for you *(Please remember I am not a guidance counselor or academic advisor, but I am offering you what I know based on my research).*

Now, let's talk about what *big fish vs. little fish* means and why so many struggle with it. Ask yourself: do you want to be a big fish in a little pond or a small fish in a big pond with all the other fishes? When I struggled with choosing a school, my dad told me to consider it seriously. Other things play into picking a school, but it never hurts to consider it.

At a smaller school, you may have the option to get started in journalism publications early on and work your way up to getting management experience. You can make some deep connections with professors, mentors, and fellow students. This could also be an option at a big school, but it may be harder to stand out. You may get lost in the crowd of students.

I would never want to guide anyone away from their dream school or the plan they already have in mind, but I wouldn't be doing you justice if I didn't tell you to consider these options. Picking a college isn't always the easiest time, but I believe that everyone will end up where they belong. Your time in high school or as a young journalist is a time to grow, make mistakes, and learn the basics of life and journalism. Anything can happen, but if you know you have a passion for the world of journalism, then nothing should stop you from pursuing it in high school.

But, college is also not for everyone. It is not the ultimate next step as a young journalist. Some people choose to go straight into the workforce, by choice or need, and skip college altogether. This is also a viable route. You can start building your resume as you'd like and maybe go to school later on. What matters is how you are growing and developing as a person first, and as a journalist second. Do what feels right for you and makes sense for where you are in the moment.

Starting journalism in your youth comes with the advantage of getting a head start on your peers on building a portfolio and resume. High school is a time to grow, make memories, and prepare for your future.

CHAPTER THIRTEEN

FOR MY COLLEGE FRIENDS

Your twenties are weird.

There—*I said it, so it is out in the open.* If your twenties live up to their nickname of the "roaring '20s," then god bless you. It is a transformative time, no matter which timeline you're on—and eventually, you and your friends do end up on different timelines. Some are in college, some are getting married, some are having babies, some are living in their parents' basements, and some are focused in on their careers. Heck, some people are doing multiple things at once.

In your twenties, you have a lot of latitude. You're encouraged to find yourself, to discover where you want to live, what you want to do, and—at the end of the day—to decide who you want to be. Then, you can change your mind, if you want.

Some young adults wrestle to discover their passions. Some wrestle to discover how to turn their passions into a livelihood. Some just seem to stumble for a while. Eventually, they stumble upon what makes them want to get out of bed in the morning. And if you haven't yet, you will, too.

The fact that you stumbled across this book leads one to suspect that you have a passion for—or at least a passing interest in—the journalism profession. You have the chance to start exactly where you are today and take steps grow into the journalist you want to be.

Start Developing Skills

If you have no previous background in journalism, there is no time like the present to start learning. Courses, whether through college or independent studies, will be key to your developing skills.

Colleges have different courses or clubs you can join to start honing your craft. Whether it's writing, editing, graphics, broadcast—whatever type of journalism you want to pursue—this is the time to try them out. Start building up your portfolio through practicing. In college courses or clubs like the newspaper, there is less pressure to be the best and more room to learn to correct mistakes.

College is also a great time to find a possible passion, niche, or interest. In your free time, what do you see yourself gravitating toward? Is it sports, fashion, different cultures, or food? Finding your niche can be easy once you find what you are passionate about. Try writing for the sports column, go to that city council meeting, or write about the town's newest restaurant.

If you have chosen a different route from college, then the Internet is your best friend. Online courses are becoming more popular as industry professionals start to take on a different teaching role. Professors are not the only ones who can teach journalism. Throw a quick search into Google, take in all the resources available, and start practicing.

You will meet an assortment of people in your twenties. There will be people from all different backgrounds of religions, lifestyles, preferences, and interests to connect with. A simple conversation with another student can turn into the profile piece of the year. This is the best time to get out there and involved in activities—talk to someone in line at the grocery store or volunteer at the retirement home. The opportunities to build a local network and find the next story are everywhere in your community. This is a great way to improve your interviewing skills, but also making connections with potential friends. Learn how to communicate with others and create an environment where people can open up to you.

Every aspiring journalist should read the news. Strike that. *Everyone* should read the news, especially aspiring journalists. A great way to learn how to write is by reading the work someone else is making a living off of right now. Pay attention to the way they structure a story, how they weave quotes into the narrative, and what it is they do to connect with the reader.

Once you feel like you have nailed the basics, you should get your name out there. Find local publications, college media, or online blogs looking for submissions. Leave behind any fears and hit the submit button. Two great options for young adults to build up their online presence are Medium and LinkedIn. These platforms allow you to post your content, engage in conversation with your online network, and get your name out there. The more you try out new things and figure out your interest, the greater your portfolio will be when applying to internships and jobs.

Young journalists create some of the most beautiful pieces, and there are people out there waiting to highlight it. Maybe one day, you'll win a Hearst Journalism Award or a College Media Association Pinnacle Award. I believe in you, and so do the people around you.

Find a Mentor

Mentors can be helpful during your young adult years. They do not always have to be someone who knows the journalism industry's ins and outs. Mentors want to see you succeed. Success does not just come from your work. It comes from how to prioritize and balance your life. Find the people who will help you when things get rough and are the first people to celebrate you when things go right. A mentor is the one that can sense things that maybe you don't want to focus on.

My sophomore year of college overwhelmed me. I found joy in filling up my Google Calendar to the max, but it got to the point that I scheduled in times to take a walk, call my parents, or even cook dinner. My life had no balance, and I quickly lost focus of my priorities. My mentor, Megan Lassiter, called me out on it.

Megan quickly became a life advisor when she joined the staff at The King's College. She helped me write my first resignation letter, but also helped me take steps toward bettering my mental health. From walks to coffee breaks in between classes, she is always ready to listen and help guide me through the things, whether it's work decisions or building up my confidence.

Your mentor may be a former boss, a professor at your school, or an industry professional. Embrace the connection you may have with someone in your life and be willing to let them help you.

If you cannot find a mentor within your community, check out Journalism Internships. Adriana Lacy created the site and program to make the journalism industry more accessible for young journalists. The website offers "paid internship, fellowship and entry-level job listings, mentoring and advice" to help shape "the future generation of media leaders [with] opportunities to make their mark on this industry, regardless of race, gender or socioeconomic status."[67]

The program's mentors volunteer their time for free sessions to discuss advice, guidance, and questions about the journalism industry. They're from all over the country, at different stages in their careers, and often have unique jobs. Mentor categories include audio and radio, data/investigative journalism, audience engagement, general reporters and editors, sports, broadcast, news design, public relations, marketing, product, and engineering.[68]

Mentors can also come from informational interviews when you reach out to someone you admire. These interviews should engage in an industry professional's career, tips, and insights. It is *not* a chance for you to ask for a job. It's a time to learn and grow and possibly make that connection. Create a list of people you find inspiring and reach out if you can find their contact information. Networking is essential to the journalism industry, and the sooner you start, the better.

LinkedIn is also a good place to connect with a mentor. But be specific and reasonable with your ask. Keep it short and professional. Why are you reaching out to this person

---

67   "Our vision," Journalism Mentors, accessed June 22, 2020.
68   "Media Mentors," Journalism Mentors, accessed June 22, 2020.

and not someone else? Mention that—don't use a generic form letter. Ask for fifteen minutes to learn more about their career journey, and learn all you can about them before you approach them. Have your questions ready in case they reply, "Okay, call me now." Include a link to your Medium blog or your portfolio. No attachments. Ask once. If you receive no reply, let it go. The news business is too small to be rude or annoying to anyone. If you do get to talk, send a thank you note no later than the next day. If the call went well and you feel confident, make another inquiry about mentorship or an internship.

Apply, Apply, Apply

When applying to internships, you'll be one of many applicants, and sometimes you will not be the first choice. *Keep* applying. If you want to pave your path, get back up when you are knocked down.

If you keep putting yourself out there and making connections, you will eventually have a breakthrough. Some of the very people who once turned you down will be the ones saying congratulations later. Your resume will fall into the right hands when the timing is right. Keep putting it out there. Your time will come.

Once you have your hand on a job description or internship description, customize your resume and cover letters to align with it. Hiring managers and employers don't need your entire work experience and trust me—they don't want it. They do want to know how you will fit best into the role. Highlight the experiences that make you the best for the role, and create custom resumes for different companies so you fit into what they are looking for. Do not waste your cover letter space and a hiring manager's time repeating what you have already in your resume. Instead, describe how you can benefit their organization, how well you can work on the team, and what you offer that's unique from other applicants.

The internet is full of detailed resources to make your application the best it can be for any type of job. Young women can begin looking at job resources and opportunities on websites like muse.com and fairygodboss.com. To find journalism job opportunities specifically, journalismjobs.com is a great place to begin a search. These websites help you discover different companies and stay connected with their openings. Learn more about the brands you are interested in, and when you are ready, jump at the opportunity to apply. And remember: one door closed means another is opening.

Your twenties are weird, but they also provide opportunities to learn new skills, make useful connections, discover your niche, develop your brand, and grow your portfolio. You may not always find yourself on the same timeline as your friends, and that's fine. Life's a journey, not a race. Plan it, and when plans change, embrace it. Uncertainty keeps you on your toes and ready to kick obstacles out of your path to continue making your own way.

CHAPTER FOURTEEN

HOW TO BE A SUPPORTER

Walk into my room and you'll notice these three things right away.

1. My three-year-old BLACK+DECKER 12-Cup Coffee Maker in the center of my tiny New York kitchenette.
2. My refrigerator covered in special notes from friends and family and the many magnets I've collected. *The pink and white "Don't mess with Texas Women" magnet from the Texas State Capitol usually catches visitor's eyes.*
3. An 80-by-68-inch wall tapestry hung prominently next to my bed proclaims: "Empowered Women, Empower Women."

Empowered women empower women. These are words to live by.

Empowered women do not seek to succeed at the expense of their sisters. They seek opportunities to support other women, just as they, too, have found support in others.

Empowered women want to empower their peers to smash goals and pursue dreams. And as they climb, empowered women turn around and lift.

I am not only speaking to women. I am talking to everyone that is a friend, family, and supporter of someone. Caring for someone means wanting them to shine and do their best. It starts with simple support.

I have found my support system among my family and friends. Sometimes people who care about us don't know we want or need support. Sometimes, people would love to support us but have no idea what to do. So, it can be helpful to communicate, "If you'd like to support me, here is how you could do that."

My career has been based on the foundational support I received from my family. I am blessed with how my parents raised me and placed an importance on me following my dreams. Not everyone will have this, which is when a support system of friends and mentors is just as vital.

My parents have always wanted me to believe I could do whatever I set my mind to. They almost expected me to reach for the stars and to push myself to get there. They have empowered me to be independent, but I know they're nearby when I need advice and support. If they think something isn't good for me, they let me know. Ultimately, they have let me make my own decisions about my future, including my choice to pursue journalism as a career.

A journalist needs a support system when they feel discouraged, burnt out, or heavyhearted. Many of us are drawn to the profession out of a sense of altruism and a desire to make a difference. In reality, while we're in the process of doing the work, we're bystanders, observing and gathering the perspective and experiences of others. When those perspectives are troubling or the experiences traumatic, it can feel like the weight of the world rests squarely on our shoulders. There are moments when journalists need a voice of reason to help guide us toward the truth and fresh eyes to help us see how deeply we're effected by our work. Sometimes we just need to be reminded why we chose to do what we do.

"I think it starts with self-reflection," Kelsey Samuels said in her 2017 TEDxPlano Talk. "I think it starts with everyone taking an introspective look at their beliefs, questioning and asking themselves, are my beliefs a reflection of the reality in front of me?"[69]

Samuels is from the North Texas area and graduated with a degree in journalism from Texas Christian University. She went on to work as a general assignment reporter for the Lufkin Daily News in East Texas and, as of 2017, now works for the Plano Star Courier as the community reporter. Samuels' "Think Like A Journalist" talk discusses how truth and realness start with going introspective.[70]

"There has to be different perspectives to this situation or even just admitting the situation isn't as simple as I think it is," Samuels closed. "It helps us make sure that our beliefs are a true reflection of the reality that we're living in and it's worth it."[71]

Samuel focused on more dealing with the Internet and "fake news" as a journalist, but her advice is also great for someone supporting a journalist in your life. This can be journalist to journalist, non-journalist to journalist, non-journalist to non-journalist. When we take a moment to put things

---

69 *Tedx Talks*, "Think Like A Journalist | Kelsey Samuels | TEDxPlano," April 26, 2017, video, 13:05.
70 *Tedx Talks*, "Think Like a Journalist."
71 Ibid.

in a different perspective, we can help each other. If we start getting into the practice of caring for what someone else is doing, we can naturally empower each other daily.

Sometimes the mind of a journalist can be confusing and overwhelming. There will be questions and knowledge circling around the stress of deadlines and new pitches. Being a supporter means helping a journalist see the reality in front of them; to remind them that their job is worth it. I want to offer up three simple tasks that will leave them feeling supported and empowered.

Ask Them Questions

Journalists can get used to always asking the questions and finding someone else's story. So much that they forget about their own. I personally love it when people ask me questions about my life. It never hurts to ask us questions and be a listener. Ask questions about our personal experiences, what we are doing at work, or if we have any plans for the future. Is there an exciting project coming up? Ask them about it and see their passion shine through.

Be Considerate of Their Work

Journalists' work often doesn't end when they leave the office. There could be a source that weighs down on them, a story that keeps them up all night, or an eagerness to simply get it done. It can take up time and energy. Like Jane said before, we can't sit here and lie and say that the journalism industry is easy. The journey is stressfully beautiful and leaves a constant mixture of eagerness and burnout behind. Support systems can help them sort through their feelings and remind them why they chose their craft in the first place.

Remember That Comments Have Big Impacts

Journalists sometimes *really* need words of affirmation. *I said it, and I don't regret it.* Our work is based on feedback from editors, sources, and the audience reading it. There is a certain level of vulnerability in publishing work, and sometimes a simple comment can go a long way. Tell us what we did well and what we can work on. Help us grow positively and help build up confidence. It shows that you took the time to reflect on our work, and you care enough to tell us. That makes a world of difference in attitude. Sometimes we just need a validation that someone is reading and seeing our work. Facebook shares, tweets, texts, and Instagram comments can go a long way.

Questions, comments, and considerations are vital in supporting a journalist or your fellow journalists. Still, I would be doing everyone a disservice if I didn't touch on topics that are actively affecting our lives. Newsrooms and companies can lack diversity in race and gender. People like Kimeko McCoy were the only woman and people of color in their newsroom at one point in their careers. We have the opportunity every day we wake up to change this. We need women to wake up and decide to be a journalist. We need black women and women of color and different cultures willing to offer their unique perspective on things. Journalism needs diversity to thrive and inform properly. How can we expect to tell the full story if we are actively ignoring parts of the story?

In 2017, the Radio Television Digital News Association (RTDNA) conducted a research study on women and minorities in newsrooms. The RTDNA focuses on promoting and protecting responsible journalism.[72] The study stated that as of 2017, the minority population in the United States had risen 12.1 points over the last twenty-seven years. The minority workforce in TV News was just at 6.6, and the minority workforce in radio was less than one point higher. This is only one section of the research.[73] Imagine what the research over time until 2020 would look like. It would look promising and revolutionary, but it would still be lackluster.

When I wrote for *Iridescent Women*, I published my article, "How to Truly Shatter the Glass Ceiling." My dad shared it on his Facebook, and someone laughed at it. They took the time to click the reactions button and chose the "haha" one to my article about shattering the glass ceiling. At eighteen, this stuck out to me.

We can preach that times are different, but people are still directly targeting any progress in the industry and our lives. Don't be this person when supporting a woman or woman of color in their journey.

I have been afforded privileges because of my skin color all of my life. It's my turn to support my fellow women and journalists and empower them just the same. If we don't, then who will? We need people who choose that every day because empowered women really do empower women. *All* women.

---

72 "About RTDNA," Radio Television Digital News Association, accessed September 21, 2020.

73 "RTDNA Research: Women and minorities in newsrooms," Bob Papper, Radio Television Digital News Association, accessed September 21, 2020.

Women deserve accurate representation and respect in newsrooms, media companies, and brands. It has improved over the years, but we are far from being done. The women mentioned in this book are some of the people still pushing forward. Women like Zoe Jones are always moving forward.

I met Zoe my freshman year of college. She is a bold woman with a bright personality. She graduated from The King's College in 2019 with a degree in media, culture, and the arts with a film and media studies concentration. Her work can be found on *Vox*, *CBS News*, *Publisher's Weekly*, *Forbes*, *Mel Magazine*, *Refinery 29*, and *Newsweek*. Zoe started working at Newsweek full-time her senior year of college following an internship and worked there until leaving to pursue freelancing opportunities.[74] Zoe introduces herself on her website as "black and bold" and is dedicated to "producing quality content about the intersection of pop culture and race."[75]

"To be honest, I've never really felt like journalism had like the biggest problem with women," Zoe commented. "In all of the newsrooms that I've been in, females and women were in really high positions of power and they were respected. But for me, I feel like I'm always black first. When people see me, it's not, 'Oh, she's a black woman.' It's 'Oh, like black.' That's the thing that comes first."

I think the industry is caught in a moment of creating an environment of representation and diversity without over-saturating it and making that someone's primary purpose. Now more than ever is when we need journalists bringing in their unique perspectives, backgrounds, and bias, but

---

74 "Portfolio," Zoe Christen Jones' Personal Website, accessed October 13, 2020.
75 "CV," Zoe Christen Jones' Personal Website, accessed October 13, 2020.

we have to remember that they are more than that. They are capable of more than just reporting what makes your publication look good. As I said in my article before, breaking the glass ceiling is when we stop identifying women as a "female politician" or "female journalist." We don't identify men as a "male politician" or "male journalists."

Zoe's breakout moment as a journalist came when she published a piece she'd written—not as a female journalist, a black journalist, or a black female journalist, but as a cousin, a niece, a member of a family who had experienced a national tragedy up close and painfully personally. Her article, "My cousin was killed in the Charleston church shootings. Here's what happens after the cameras leave," captured her unfiltered emotions. It also brought attention to Zoe and her work. She originally published the article on Medium, and after it gained attention, Vox republished it as well. The trajectory of her career may have changed, but her need for a strong emotional support system has not. Fortunately, Zoe has that. When we talked recently about the experience, she offered this advice to those who want to know how to support the journalists in what they do.

"I would say that you don't have to make their life harder," Zoe said. "They already know that they're missing something, or they already know that they're reporting tough stuff, but if it's what they want to do, then you just have to love them as best you can."

Zoe recalled how her friends, rather than being upset she couldn't make their nights out, started going to places near her office so she could come and go as she pleased. They didn't mock her when she would bring her laptop to dinner. They called her out when she was overworking and supported her when she decided to quit her job to start freelancing.

In the end, we are all human, and we all need a support system. Life is happening all around us. We were made for community and to be there for each other. Supporting a journalist is defending the truth and sharing stories. Every single person has their own information. We can learn from each other and support each other in life as we reflect on what is going on introspectively. Are you happy with what you see? Are you ready to change your life? You are surrounded by people with unique stories waiting to be shared with the world.

Are you ready to go beyond the title to find the story and be a storyteller?

APPENDIX

Epigraph

Salemi, Vicki. ""Shonda Rhimes on Writing in the Age of Trump: 'TV Has Power. My Pen Has Power.'" *Vulture*, November 22, 2016. https://www.vulture.com/2016/11/shonda-rhimes-tv-has-power-my-pen-has-power.html

Chapter 1

American Press Institute. "About Us." Accessed June 9, 2020. https://www.americanpressinstitute.org/about/about-us/

Bilton, Luke. "Kate Adie: 'I Never Desired to Go into War Zones. It Just Sort of Happened as Part of the Job.'" *IFSEC Global*, March 17, 2016. https://www.ifsecglobal.com/global/kate-adie-i-never-desired-to-go-into-war-zones-it-sort-of-just-happened-as-part-of-the-job/

Katie Adie's Official Website. "Books." Accessed June 9, 2020. http://kateadie.co.uk/books.htm

USHistory.org. "The Trial of John Peter Zenger." Accessed September 30, 2020. http://www.ushistory.org/us/7c.asp

Chapter 2

Merriam-Webster.com Dictionary, s.v. "Clickbait." Accessed August 22, 2020. https://www.merriam-webster.com/dictionary/clickbait

TEDx Talks. "The Power of Digital Journalism | Anita Li | TEDx DistilleryDistrictWomen." August 5, 2015. Video, 8:42. https://www.youtube.com/watch?v=nhrZHRqUaTo&list=WL&index=50

Chapter 4

Her Campus Media. "About." Accessed June 19, 2020. https://www.hercampusmedia.com/about
Her Campus. "About Us." Accessed June 19, 2020. https://www.hercampus.com/about-us

Chapter 5

American Society of Magazine Editors. "Winners of 2017 ASME Next Awards Announced." Published February 2, 2017. https://www.asme.media/winners-2017-asme-next-awards-announced
Clout Coffee. "About Clout." Accessed September 30, 2020. https://www.cloutcoffee.com/pages/about-clout
Edge Magazine. "About Us." Accessed June 21, 2020. http://edgemagazine.com/about-us/
Forbes Media. "Lindsay Peoples Wagner, 29." Accessed June 19, 2020. https://www.forbes.com/pictures/5ddb2959e0af7b0006b2374a/lindsay-peoples-wagner-29/

Hosbeg (Blog). "Difference Between Online and Print Journalism." Accessed May 11, 2020. https://hosbeg.com/difference-between-online-and-print-journalism/

LinkedIn. "Carole Sprunk." Accessed June 21, 2020. https://www.linkedin.com/in/carolesprunk/

LinkedIn. "Lindsay Peoples Wagner." Accessed June 19, 2020. https://www.linkedin.com/in/lindsayp/

Teen Vogue. "Teen Vogue's Editor-In-Chief Explains Her Career Path, from First Job to Current | Teen Vogue." August 22, 2019. Video, 11:58. https://www.youtube.com/watch?v=vmOJPACojoc

Chapter 6

Alissa Wilkinson. "About." Accessed June 20, 2020. http://www.alissawilkinson.com/

Iridescent Women (Blog). "About Us." Accessed October 11, 2020. https://iridescentwomen.com/aboutus/

Iridescent Women (Blog). "Iridescent Values." Accessed May 10, 2020. https://iridescentwomen.com/values/

Chapter 7

Journalism Mentors. "Media Mentors: Audience Engagement." Accessed June 21, 2020. https://journalismmentors.com/mentors/audience-engagement

Lacy, Adriana. Journalism Mentors. "Introducing Media Mentors." Published October 16, 2019. Accessed June 21, 2020. https://journalismmentors.com/the-blog/introducing-media-mentors

LinkedIn. "Kimeko McCoy." Accessed June 21, 2020. https://www.linkedin.com/in/kimeko-mccoy-2018/

Rotten Tomatoes. "Breakfast at Tiffany's Quotes." Accessed October 25, 2020. https://www.rottentomatoes.com/m/breakfast_at_tiffanys/quotes/

Chapter 8

ABC News. "Telling legendary journalist Marie Colvin's story in 'A Private War.'" November 8, 2018. Video, 8:29. https://www.youtube.com/watch?v=vdOPRLykvFA

Fulbright Program. "About." Accessed May 10, 2020. https://us.fulbrightonline.org/about

Goodreads. "Benjamin Mee." Accessed June 20, 2020. https://www.goodreads.com/author/show/1350576.Benjamin_Mee

Hilsum, Lindsey. "Marie Colvin—the making of a myth." *Financial Times*, February 5, 2019. https://www.ft.com/content/c72c571c-260f-11e9-8ce6-5db4543da632

Marie Colvin Memorial Foundation. "Marie's Story." Accessed October 1, 2020. https://mariecolvin.org/about-marie1

Marie Colvin Memorial Foundation. "Truth at All Costs." Accessed October 1, 2020. https://mariecolvin.org/truth-at-all-costs-marie-colvin

Plano, Catherine. "Twenty Seconds of Insane Courage…." *Medium* (blog), November 10, 2019. https://medium.com/@catherine_40404/twenty-seconds-of-insane-courage-d81bd774e34e

Chapter 9

Condé Nast. "Glamour." Accessed October 1, 2020. https://www.condenast.com/brands/glamour/

FLIK. "Mission." Accessed October 1, 2020. https://weareflik.com/mission

Glamour. "Women of the Year." Accessed October 1, 2020. https://www.glamour.com/inspired/women-of-the-year

The Leading Ladies at FLIK. "5 Chapters w/ Samantha Barry (Editor-in-Chief of Glamour)." November 6, 2019. Video, 7:03. https://www.youtube.com/watch?v=ibW5cKjwSFY

Chapter 10

Ciobanu, Mădălina. "'Women on air' discuss the importance of confidence and mentoring to succeed in the media industry." *Journalism.co.uk*, June 1, 2016. https://www.journalism.co.uk/news/mentors-and-confidence-advice-from-and-for-female-journalists-working-in-broadcasting/s2/a642847/

The Southern Social. "FAQ." Accessed June 18, 2020. https://www.thesouthernsocialtx.com/faq

Chapter 11

CBS News. "Katie's advice for aspiring journalists." February 25, 2011. Video, 4:31. https://www.youtube.com/watch?v=8n4Toigeh6I

Katie Couric Media. "About Katie Couric." Accessed October 26, 2020. https://katiecouric.com/about-katie-couric/

Katie Couric Media. "About KCM." Accessed June 21, 2020. https://katiecouric.com/about-kcm/

LinkedIn. "Katie Couric." Accessed June 21, 2020. https://www.linkedin.com/in/katiecouric/

Chapter 12

Tedx Talks. "Empowerment Through Youth Journalism | Natalie Bettendorf | TEDxYouth@EB." December 14, 2016. Video, 15:15. https://www.youtube.com/watch?v=6AjlyV1xebk

Chapter 13

Journalism Mentors. "Media Mentors." Accessed June 22, 2020. https://journalismmentors.com/mentors

Journalism Mentors. "Our Vision." Accessed June 22, 2020. https://journalismmentors.com/our-vision

Chapter 14

Papper, Bob. Radio Television Digital News Association. "RTDNA Research: Women and minorities in newsrooms." Accessed September 21, 2020.

Radio Television Digital News Association. "About RTDNA." Accessed September 21, 2020. https://www.rtdna.org/content/about_rtdna

Tedx Talks. "Think Like A Journalist | Kelsey Samuels | TEDxPlano." April 26, 2017. Video, 13:05. https://www.youtube.com/watch?v=09rBZ5FwFjw&t=643s

Zoe Christen Jones' Personal Website. "CV." Accessed October 13, 2020. https://www.zoechristenjones.com/cv

Zoe Christen Jones' Personal Website. "Portfolio." Accessed October 13, 2020. https://www.zoechristenjones.com/portfolio

ACKNOWLEDGMENTS

Writing a book is a multitude of processes and feelings. Ones that you may not account for when you sign up for it. There were more challenging and humbling moments than I could have imagined, but this whole process would not have been possible without the support all around me. Each and every conversation for the book and about the book taught me something new about life. The people around me are the reason why this book is a reality. Because of these people, I, along with all of the women featured in this book, can continue to share our stories and offer something new to the world. Here are the people who have been a part of my journey:

First and foremost, thank you to all of my interviewees for sharing your stories and your passion with me during unprecedented times. Your stories have inspired me, and it's a great honor to share them with others. Thank you Carole, Melissa, Shannon, Nicole, Christiana, Kimeko, Serena, and Zoe. Thanks also to your family members and friends—Joanne Mason, Suzanne Mason, Carolyne Nielson, and Sandra Colclough—for the support.

Thank you to my family. I have never felt unprepared to take on any challenge thrown in my direction because of y'all. Mom and Dad, thank you for always pushing me to strive to discover my true passions in life and to dream beyond what society has told me. To my brother, Ryan, thank you for being my number one fan and for always looking out for me.

Thank you to the rest of my family. We may be small, but your love and support is very mighty. Thank you Larry and Lineth, Aunt Debra, Uncle Rick, Sara, and Cody, Papa, Grandma, Heather, and Morgan for championing me every step of the way.

Thank you to my friends from my hometown, journalism camps, and Texas Girls State: Reagan Jones, Laney White, Maddie Badowski, Brice Corbin, AP Velasco, Courtney Hudson, Addie Angelo, Heather Martin, and Mashayla Marler. Thank you as well to Kristen Mills for helping me realize my passion for empowerment as a citizen of Texas Bluebonnet Girls State, and for your continuing support.

Thank you to my friends and college professors in NYC: Sam Klozik, Alissa Wilkinson, LG Pannell, Jolie Richardson, Deborah Gonçalves, Catherine Blanco, Montgomery Drumm, Ellen Coy, Abby Miller, Hope Villandre, Hannah Sarenpa, Mckenna Morgan, Juliette Kheyfets, Lauren Williams, Tia McCord, Neidín Shelnutt, Leticia Mosqueda, Joshua Hershey, and Rachel Freeman.

Thank you Megan Lassiter for helping me overcome every obstacle along this journey. You've been a vital part of my support system since the day you walked into my life, and your support means the world.

To my best friend, Kennedy, thank you for your continuous support and encouragement. I'm blessed that the city brought us together and we get to live out our childhood dreams at the same time.

Thank you to the people of Midlothian that have supported me throughout my life at different points and didn't shy away from showing their support for the book. Thank you Jeanette Ponce, Sue McKenrick, Sarah Reynolds, Gaby Galicia, Alicia Coomes, Laurie Lundberg, Taylor Avaritt, Stacy Gardner, The Phillips Family, Carole and Bill Mccarley, Joe Don Cavender, Christi Corbin, Shannon and Jimmy Beaudoin, Karson Conrad, Cathy Altman, Trisha Phillips, and The McKay family.

I have always said I am a proud product of the Midlothian Independent School District, and the support I have received from my former mentors and teachers has meant the world to me. Thank you Bethany Shields, Jennifer Ferranti, Megan Ross, David Moore, Lorilyn Worley, Geri Salazar, Ronnie Gail Hamilton, Aaron Gabrysch, Joyce Griffith, Riki Underwood, Melonie Bagby, Beth Stewart, Ellen Hayden, Aly Gaither, The Strueby's, Jill Schaben, Meredith Bunch, and Monica Wolf.

A massive thank you goes to New Degree Press and Creator Institute for taking my dream from thought to reality. Thank you Eric Koester, Brian Bies, Jacqueline Diaz-Mewes,

P. Richelle White, Leila Summers, and everyone else who played a role in publishing this book.

Lastly, I say thank you to my inspirations for living my life to the fullest and part of the reason why I took a chance on writing my own book. To my Uncle Milton and Granny, I hope you are watching down on me and are so very proud of my accomplishment. I wish you were here to enjoy this moment with me, but your love and memory helped this book be published.

Printed in Great Britain
by Amazon